Questions of Identity:

A Selection from the Pages of *New European*

Questions of Identity:

A Selection from the Pages of *New European*

Edited and with an introduction by

Christopher Joyce

I.B.Tauris *Publishers*
LONDON • NEW YORK

in association with

NEW EUROPEAN PUBLICATIONS LONDON

Published in 2002 by I.B.Tauris & Co Ltd
6 Salem Road, London W2 4BU
175 Fifth Avenue, New York NY 10010
www.ibtauris.com

In the United States of America and in Canada distributed by
Palgrave Macmillan a division of St Martins Press
175 Fifth Avenue, New York NY 10010

ISBN 1 86064 696 4

A full CIP record for this book is available from the British Library
A full CIP record for this book is available from the Library of Congress

Library of Congress catalog card: available

Typeset in Garamond and Perpetua by www.orbitgraphic.co.uk
Printed and bound in Great Britain by MPG Books Ltd, Bodmin

Contents

Introduction vii

1. Powerful People in the New Europe 1
   George Bull, 1991.

2. Enlargement of the European Union, Challenge
   and Chance – an Austrian Perspective 7
   Dr Erhard Busek, 2000.

3. Political Union in Europe 15
   Ronald Butt, 1990.

4. Safeguarding the British Constitution 25
   Ronald Butt, 1990.

5. A 19th Century View of Europe – Is it still the same? 35
   John Coleman, 1991.

6. Money, Politics and Europe 45
   Ralf Dahrendorf, 1990.

7. Europe Must Avoid the American Model 59
   Janet Daley, 1989.

8. 1988 – Britain's Year of the Dutch 65
   Christie Davies, 1989.

9. **The Future of Europe** 69
Ted Dunn, 1989.

10. **Is Mrs Thatcher's Europe Realisable?** 77
Douglas Evans, 1989.

11. **Beyond Götterdämmerung – Europe's Preparation
for the Twenty-first Century** 85
Noriko Hama, 1994.

12. **Ideas about an 'Idea of Europe'** 93
Richard Hoggart & Douglas Johnson, 1988.

13. **The Price of Union** 101
David Howell, 1989.

14. **Europe of the Mind** 105
Michael Ignatieff, 1988.

15. **The European Tapestry of Nations** 115
Flora Lewis, 1989.

16. **Fresh Interest in European Civilization** 121
C.A.O. van Nieuwenhuijze, 1989.

17. **My Ten Most European Experiences** 129
Cees Nooteboom, 1988.

18. **Nigeria and Europe: not so distant cousins** 137
Dele Oguntimoju, 2000.

19. **European Thoughts from Aquitaine** 145
Kenneth Leech Pearson, 1989.

20. **Symposium on the Wider Europe
and the Wider World** 151
Enoch Powell, 1989.

21. **Perceiving the Uncomfortable Patterns** 159
Enoch Powell, 1988.

22. **The Official Version** 163
Aidan Rankin, 2000.

Contents

23. Europe, America and Asia   173
    Geoffrey Rippon, 1989.

24. The Representation of UK Interests in Europe   179
    Ann Robinson, 1989.

25. A Question of Identity   191
    Philip Schlesinger, 1989.

26. Britain's European Heritage   199
    Norman Stone, 1990.

27. European Family of Nations   205
    Margaret Thatcher, 1989.

28. The Real Questions for Europe   217
    Christopher Tugendhat, 1989.

29. Deeper and Wider   225
    Ernest Wistrich, 1992.

Introduction

New European began to appear a little over ten years ago. Ten years in politics is a very long time, but a persistent underlying theme has marked the 'debate' about 'Europe' throughout this period. That theme, in a word, is 'identity'. Three sets of inverted commas. Let us take them in reverse order. 'Identity'. What does it mean to say one is French (or German or Dutch, or any other nationality)? What does it – and might it – mean to say one is European? 'Europe'. What would be the real consequences of further European integration? Could there be an hiatus between *machinery* of integration and how people felt about its effects? Or could a European (that is to say a citizen of one of the member states of the European Union) become a 'European' (a citizen of a unified European state) without realising that this had happened? Some readers may be unsure as to which of these two senses of 'European' should bear the inverted commas; but these would of course be redundant if the distinction were removed. Lastly, 'debate'. The founders of *New European* asked themselves whether there had really been a debate about Europe. A good deal of heat had been generated, certainly; but perhaps not so much light.

Parliamentary debate in Britain there had been, most famously – or infamously, depending on how one viewed it – the debate on the Second Reading of the European Communities Bill (the paving legislation for accession to the European Treaties) some 15 years earlier. Here is how the late Lord Jay described its closing stage on the night of 17 February 1972:

"The result was a vote for the Second Reading by only 309 votes to 301. So this constitutional revolution was imposed on us by only eight votes in 600... This was to me the most tragic moment in the whole story. So much vast effort had been made for so long by the opponents of the Bill to defeat it at this stage; and despite the huge propaganda resources, and all the influence of the Government ranged against them, they had only failed by this tiny margin of eight votes. Feeling – genuine, deep and almost uncontrolled – erupted around the Chamber and particularly on the Labour benches near me... It was the fiercest moment in the House since Suez."

Even for people who were 'around at the time' it is difficult now to recall the passion – and the invective – which the European issue called up in those now distant days, and impossible for anyone younger than about 45 now. And it was that passion and invective rather than reason and reflection that continued to dominate the debate for some years to come.

This was the situation on which *New European* impinged. Not that it was ever assumed that politics could or should be passionless. Quite the reverse. That is why the new journal gave a good deal of space to exploring questions of identity: what sort of community might Europe be, conceived as a community concerned with more than reciprocal trading arrangements, and what might 'belonging' to it mean? But it was (and remains) part of the credo of *New European* that a period of genuine reflection, of political, social and intellectual enquiry, was much overdue, and that a passion could be tempered by reason. The title of Michael Ignatieff's contribution to the first number (Winter 1987-88) – 'Europe of the Mind' – encapsulated an idea which informed the development of the journal from the start. Ignatieff saw the European Community (as it then was) as its own worst enemy: "The Community process," he writes, "has confiscated the energy and commitment behind the cultural idea of Europe and turned the word 'Europe' into a thought-stopping bore, evoking only the grey round of Ministerial meetings in concrete bunkers in Strasbourg and Brussels. The debate about Britain's role in Europe...is a debate about what kind of identity Britain can make for itself in the re-discovery that it has been a European society all along."

If that debate had "hardly started" ten years ago, as Ignatieff believed, it is now – and rightly – *in volle gegang*; and and much of the credit for this must surely go to *New European*. In a steady stream of articles and reviews from many different perspectives the issues that Ignatieff identified have been explored, analysed and discussed. *New European* recognised that there could be no worthwhile attempt to discern the patterns of change in the social and political climate without a well-informed view of the present realities both in Europe and globally. This also meant a well-informed view of the past, for as Richard Hoggart and Douglas Johnson remark in 'Ideas about an 'Idea of Europe'', "without a sense of history there is little sense of the future or of destiny, as Europeans fail to create significant intellectual movements and decay into a society dominated by consumerism, servicing and leisure."

The term 'intellectual movement' aptly suggests the driving force behind *New European,* for there has been no attempt to straitjacket the issues – no manifesto or sub-text beyond a desire to 'saturate politics with thought' (as Mathew Arnold said of Burke). At the end of its first decade *New European* had published more than 200 contributions from the pens of politicians, economists, members of the business community, historians, journalists, environmentalists and many others. Illuminating, thoughtful, lively, eloquent, blunt...the following pieces can be variously described. But as a collection they make essential reading for anyone who wants to do some real thinking about the issues (rather than merely sounding off about them) or wants to acquire a solid basis for opinion instead of floundering in a sea of uncertainty.

A selection such as this, focused on the theme of identity, cannot give a true cross-section of these multiple perspectives: several other selections could be made from quarterly issues that now form a substantial library of information, opinion and debate. Still less is it possible in a short introduction to do justice to the remarkable range and diversity of viewpoints that *New European* has embraced within a coherent framework over the last ten years. But even in the present selection, they are well illustrated by comparing and contrasting Christopher Tugendhat's contribution to the symposium on Europe's future – 'The Real Questions for Europe' – with David Howell's – 'The Price of Union'. Or read Flora Lewis's 'The European Tapestry of Nations' alongside Margaret Thatcher's 'The European Family of Nations'. Perhaps as the former says of Margaret Thatcher and Jacques Delor, "they aren't as far apart as they sound"! And it is a salutary reminder of the rapidity of change that writing only a little more than a decade ago – in the Winter issue of 1989/90 – Mrs Thatcher could exhort us "never to forget that East of the Iron Curtain peoples who once enjoyed a full share of European culture, freedom and identity have been cut off from their roots."

For, with remarkable prescience, Enoch Powell in an earlier issue had written: "The arrival of Mr. Gorbachov at Brize Norton in December 1987 signalised another profound re-arrangement, which is now taking place under our noses and which will leave little unchanged in international – or, for that matter, in national – politics. We are witnessing the dissolution of that dual pattern of North Atlantic Alliance versus Warsaw Pact which anyone alive today under the age of 40 was born into regarding as only slightly less permanent than the solar system." Only slightly less permanent than the solar system – perhaps that should be a warning also to those of us inclined to believe the same of the present political and economic configuration of Europe. We need to be alert to the habit events have in politics, as much as in our personal lives, of not turning out as we expect them to. When setting out on a journey – or not missing the train, as it is sometimes called – it may be helpful to know at least the general direction in which we are travelling, and that one can change course if need be.

But to return to history and to culture. Turn up 'My ten most European Experiences' by the great Dutch travel writer and poet, lover of Spain and of the Classical South, Cees Nooteboom. In these vivid vignettes we see restored that "confiscated energy and commitment behind the cultural idea of Europe" which Ignatieff lamented. Do not copy the North, he tells his Mediterranean friends, "in its pursuit of soul-less modernity." Is this advice which can be absorbed into the practical politics of Europe? How shall we balance disparity and convergence, likeness and difference, continuity and change? These are not, as they may at first appear, rarefied questions that belong to the margin we reserve for cultural and artistic adornments to the real business of life. They are pressingly real questions on which the 'grey round of Ministerial meetings in concrete bunkers' may eventually founder if they remain ignored for too long. Even before the advent of a single currency, the single market is under strain. There are multi-faceted questions examined from many angles in these pages: by Kenneth Leech Pearson, for example, in his 'European Thoughts from Aquitaine', by Norman Stone in 'Britain's European Heritage', by Philip Schlesinger in 'A question of Identity', and Janet Daley in 'Europe must avoid the American Model', by Peter Cannon-Brookes in 'Strength in Diversity', by Ernest Wistrich in 'Deeper and Wider', and by many other hands.

The ramifications of 'identity' extend to every dimension of the European question. They are searchingly – if not abrasively – explored by Ronald Butt in his article 'Safeguarding the British Constitution' in which he urges those who advocate a federal Europe to "say so candidly and explain in detail what proposals they have to make it politically accountable." He is surely right that "it would at least be a step towards the answers if we openly discussed the questions". They are explored indirectly by Geoffrey Rippon in the context of Britain's global trading arrangements: see his 'Europe, America and Asia' (part of a symposium on 'The wider Europe and the wider World'). Lord Rippon's perspective is especially interesting in view of his key role under Ted Heath's premiership in negotiating the terms of British accession.

Enlisting Mrs Thatcher as an ally in the cause of a common future that "does not lie only in Europe", he seeks to define a position in which "close trading and political relations with America, Asia and the rest of the world are complementary and not contradictory to what we seek to achieve in our own continent." And here is a point at which to remind the reader of the need – in these pages and in the debate more generally – for vigilant thought about the nature of language, about how we interpret a writer's vocabulary; for a 'common future' depends on a common understanding of the words we use to define it. Lord Rippon's sword has an ironical edge: "In Britain we are frequently suspicious of the sort of harmonisation that might compel us to drink 'Euro-beer' or worse still, to eat a 'Euro-sausage'. We happen to like our sausages to be mostly fried bread in a skin. After all, as the Chinese proverb says: 'What is patriotism but a nostalgia for the food one ate as a child.' Readers will no doubt supply their own answers.

Looking back to an earlier episode in Britain's relations with the emerging European idea, Edmund Dell suggests convincingly that the United Kingdom had – and missed – its major opportunity to influence the shape of the new Europe as far back as the time of the Schumann Plan. It was at this stage, now nearly half a century ago, that Britain 'missed the boat', not during the arguments of the Macmillan and Wilson eras on the merits or otherwise of 'Common Market' membership. He attributes this failure to the then Foreign Secretary, Ernest Bevin – "a great man long past it" – who, through illness, pride, lack of foresight, and a distinct dash of Francophobia, refused UK participation in the negotiations to set up the Coal and Steel Community. The Foreign Office mandarins come "a good second" in culpability. The outcome: "irreparable and unnecessary damage to British influence on the character of European integration and to British relations with France and Western Europe."

The relationship of the national to the supranational is highly germane to the newly liberated states of Central and Eastern Europe – witness Vaclav Havel's 'Europe – the Letter or the Spirit'. His arguments are the more compelling on account of his evident sympathy for the idea of European unity. He wrestles with the problem of how the ends and values which should inform the idea – the 'spirit of unity' – shall not be lost in the preoccupation with political machinery and its functioning. Havel's plea to the West is complemented by Sergiu Celac's 'Diplomacy in a Time of Transition'. Celac – then Romanian ambassador in London – appeals in essence for multiple Europes, or (one might say) a Europe of fluid and continuously overlapping pools of interest: a figurative or conceptual counterpart to the infinitely complex and dynamic Europe of practical political realities. Diplomacy, he recognises, has a vital role in "working towards desirable futures" – a more worthwhile exercise, he notes, than merely constructing scenarios (almost invariably wrong) out of historic trends. There is an echo of Powell here: "Probably the most glaring is the dismal failure of all Kremlin-watchers and experts on East European satrapies to predict what actually happened four years ago." But we have a sudden sharp reminder of the ethos of life behind the Iron Curtain – and perhaps of its built-in guarantee of eventual failure – when Celac tells us: "During my 12 years of internal exile, I was happy when I could lay my hands on an old copy of

Times or *Newsweek* once every six months. In communist times diplomats were among the privileged few who had exposure to Western values and information."

To see the 'idea' of Europe through the eyes of a Celac or a Havel is to gain a new oversight; for acceptance of the Central and Eastern European states into the 'European family of nations' is in a sense their *Westpolitik*, with a force of history behind it very different from our own. With the Czech Republic among the latest tranche of applicants waiting in the wings of membership – along with Cyprus, Slovenia, Hungary, Poland and Estonia – the complex balance of tensions within the European institutional structure will most certainly call for an unprecedented exercise of political skill and commitment. On a slower track come Bulgaria, Romania, Slovakia, and the remaining two Baltic states, Latvia and Lithuania. And the vexed question of Turkey will not lie down.

The problem of identity, though in different guise, also permeates the issues surrounding the economic prospects of a more closely integrated Europe. Ann Robinson concludes that in the 21st century we shall want a Europe which is "less Napoleonic in outlook", one in which the political leaders "respond much more to the legitimate concerns of the people who elected them" and take a clearer line on its future shape and powers. Whether or not it was *àpropos* that the figure of Eddie George should have stepped out from behind the forbidding façade of the Bank of England (becoming almost a television celebrity overnight) during Kenneth Clarke's tenure at the Treasury, *New European* was pleased to publish his thoughtful and informed view of the prospects for European Monetary Union. Since the ERM débâcle it had become even more urgent to promote a period – perhaps a lengthy one – of careful and detailed reflection. Even by financial criteria the arguments were far from clear-cut; and, as Eddie George points out, the decision must be essentially a political one: ultimately a decision that the people themselves have to make if their politicians will allow them.

Supplying the political dimension is Nigel Lawson in a characteristically robust and searching piece in the next issue of *New European*. There he saw "no reason whatever why, with the UK outside a European monetary union, the City of London should lose its position as the financial capital of Europe and one of the three great financial centres of the world." But he saw every reason why before entering into monetary union "the precise details of the political union which is its essential counterpart and underpinning need to be spelled out and agreed." Anyone seeking an alternative construction on broadly the same 'data' – a different way of looking at the world, one might say – could hardly do better than to read Ralph Dahrendorf's incisive essay, 'Money, Politics and Europe'. Lord Dahrendorf is "not dreaming of a European superstate." For him the attraction of monetary union and its political counterpart lies in their providing "a zone of stability", which, he believes, can be achieved without detriment to those aspects of sovereignty which have not, for reasons outside the control of government, already "left national shores and borders."

Between them, these three – a pre-eminent national banker, a former Chancellor of the Exchequer and a distinguished political scientist – cover as wide a canvas as most readers will hope for. Few will come away without being much better equipped to argue the pros and cons, as we shall all need to imminently.

But perhaps the most remarkable article that *New European* has yet published is Noriko Hama's 'Beyond Götterdämmerung – Europe's preparation for the 21st Century'. "Twilight," she observes, "seems…to cast deep gloom on the turn of the century Europe." Yet there may still be hope, "for as Hegel would have us know, Minerva's owl of wisdom takes flight at dusk." Like Noriko Hama, *New European* is "fascinated by Minerva's messenger" and "what form that messenger will take for today's Europe."

The following pages do not reveal the future but they *do* identify and address some of the crucial questions that need to be 'openly discussed' if tomorrow's Europe is to be founded on genuine wisdom in contrast to mere commercial expediency (or its apparition) and political coercion, its lacky. But the book is not simply a series of snapshots in time. It shows the evolution of a debate and the unfolding of events, and the symbiotic relationship between the two. We cannot know what the next ten years' history will disclose, but we can be well or poorly prepared to shape it. As George Bull says: "We need not be so severe as Acton, and we can assume that power may be well used or badly used as we examine it in context of current European development. In Britain, Mr Hague's more sharply delineated position than his predecessors – "in Europe, but not run by Europe" – failed to swing the electorate in his party's favour. However it has concentrated minds and strikes a chord well beyond the Conservative Party. 'New Labour' has yet to respond to it clearly and events are perhaps now only starting to reveal how it will respond to the wider challenge of 'Europe'.

November 2001

Note on the Editor

Christopher Joyce is a former civil servant with a long-standing interest in European Affairs and experience of the workings of the Community. He holds degrees from Cambridge and Reading Universities and is currently an Associate Lecturer in the University of Surrey.

1

Powerful People in the New Europe

George Bull, 1991.

George Bull is one of the leading Classical scholars of the twentieth century and was Editor of **International Minds**.

AS the debate over the future constitution of the European Community grows more intense in the run-up to the Maastricht Summit in December, I hope that more attention is paid to questions of power and personality. Worries about the abuse of power, especially as it becomes more concentrated, and about evil leadership, are familiar to all of us. We do not need to be able to quote Lord Acton, but his famous dictum is always worth accurate repetition. Acton was writing to Bishop Creighton in the context of his review of Creighton's *History of the Papacy*, published in 1882. He applies his severe doctrine of public morality to the behaviour of the Popes; after arguing about the individual and collective responsibility of medieval and Renaissance Popes, he continues:

> ... I cannot accept your canon that we are to judge Pope and King unlike other men, with a favourable assumption that they did no wrong. If there is any presumption, it is the other way, against the holders of power, increasing as the power increases.

1

Historic responsibility has to make up for the want of legal responsibility. Power tends to corrupt, and absolute power corrupts absolutely. Great men are almost always bad men, even when they exercise influence and not authority, still more when you superadd the tendency or the certainty of corruption by authority...

A great deal of the discussion about the desirability of greater political and financial collaboration in the European Community has been indirectly about power, but the word itself has rarely been used and the dangers of the concentration of power have not been aired to any noticeable extent. The argument has tended to be about political structures and the meaning of "sovereignty". Thus in a recent contribution to *The Tablet* weekly publication, Sir Michael Pike (till recently British High Commissioner in Singapore) talked enthusiastically of the "transcending" of nationalism by the:

> most important new political idea...which the West has invented since 1945: the slow, unsure, fiercely contested, yet probably historically inevitable, creation of a new type of entity, economically integrated, politically diverse, subject to constant change and growth, yet always evolving by consent.

In the context of the bitter conflicts of Yugoslavia, Pike insists that for the sake of the new, emerging Europe, "the Community should now declare that it is strongly opposed in principle to the creation of new sovereign states in Europe..." Yugoslavia must be encouraged to establish a new kind of polity, still sovereign but looser in structure, and so too must the fragmenting Soviet Union. If we are to encourage not only a federation but a confederation of Europe, we shall need to be rather more clear about the nature and distribution of power in the new polity. So far, references to "subsidiarity" have been rather confused and imprecise. In Sir Richard Body's *Europe of Many Circles*, the question of power does indeed feature prominently in the last chapter where we are asked to consider *whether* the shifts proposed for Europe will mean concentrating power in fewer hands, *who* is seeking the shift in power, and *why* this shift is being sought. There is a suggestion of conspiracy which makes me feel uneasy; but I am even more persuaded that these and many more questions about power in the "new Europe" must be vigorously pursued by the pleas of people such as Tomaz Mastnak and Lynne Jones (writing about Yugoslavia in *The Times* Literary Supplement of 19 July 1991) that:

> the creation of new independent states, whether in the Baltics or Balkans, need not reduce the prospects for European integration. It is the smaller nations who…are pushing for a new vision of Europe…where power is devolved to the smallest unit and co-operation is enhanced at every level…

Acton did not write in abstract moralistic terms when he warned about the corrupting effects of power and especially great power. A devout Catholic, he pointed his finger not only at Sixtus IV but also – because of the "general wickedness of men in authority" – at Henry VIII, Philip II, Queen Elizabeth, too, and Cromwell. The new Europe, whatever its constitution, is already seeing a greater concentration of power not in the abstract but in the hands of particular bodies and people. It is time to follow this process far more intently than has been done so far. How much thought are we giving to the sort of leaders, presumably elected, who will, in Milton's strong phrase, "mould the sufferance and subjection of the people to the length of that foot that is to tread on their necks …"? There seems to be an unspoken assumption that in a more united, perhaps federal, and democratic Europe, we need not fear that power may hideously corrupt. But in our time above all we have evidence of the compatibility of a democratic system with base dictatorial ambitions, at least in their early stages, as when the National Socialists became the second largest party in the Reichstag in 1930.

Lord Bullock recently published a timely reminder of the rise to power and the traits of personality of Hitler and Stalin: an ingenious dual biography not to the liking of those who believe that individuals count for very little in the long march of history. The book reminds us that the two tyrants had millions of supporters and reached power within existing state machines. The premature deaths for which Acton at least would hold them morally accountable ran, and we need no reminding, to tens of millions.

In correspondence with me over the importance of psychological studies (both of nations and of individuals) to the conduct of diplomacy and the understanding of international affairs, Lord Bullock commented that, given that we might have been able to obtain early psychological perceptions of the minds of Hitler and Stalin, he did not see that this made it at all clear what might have been done about it. It is difficult to test the truth of this thoughtful scepticism, among other reasons because psychologists have not rushed to write about international affairs (even since Graham Wallas challenged them in 1908 with the remark that "nearly all students of politics analyse institutions and avoid the analysis of man… The study of human nature by the psychologists…has advanced without affecting or being affected by the study of politics"). Diplomats, British diplomats certainly – notwithstanding being asked for the benefit of their expertise by East European governments – are not trained to pursue psychological understanding in their work at any stage of their career. The search for understanding is invariably made too crudely and too late by governments as an addition to "intelligence" or propaganda, and with little attention to shared responsibilities. No doubt some measure of understanding is often sought by the world's statesmen and by many envoys. But this has not been to the extent that enabled them to foresee the momentous changes in East Europe or the Soviet Union occurring in 1989 or, say, the reactions of Saddam Hussein to the circumstances which led up to his attack on Kuwait and have since sustained his prestige in many quarters of the world. And we cannot think what to do about mad or bad rulers or ominous developments within peoples unless we discern them.

In business life, more and more attention is paid to the role of the failure of management at all levels in accidents and disasters and the tremendous impact on corporate success or failure of single human beings in positions of considerable power. In my hopes for a peaceful, free and creative Europe, I urge people to think harder about power in the Community and who will wield it, and about how we can monitor the effects of growing centralisation on our different peoples' fears and hopes: the English and French, proud of being the oldest nation states in Europe; the Germans with their unifying language; the Italians used to despising the state, loving the *campanile* and yearning for the Holy Roman Empire... Above all, let us start looking harder at the business leaders, bureaucrats and politicians – *nos semblables, nos freres* – who will be leading the advance towards a federal Europe through the Maastricht gap. It was the head of the great federal democracy of America, President Kennedy, who pulled wool over people's eyes with collusion from those sharing power with him as skilfully if not as disastrously as Hitler and Stalin.

When Michael Heseltine said to Nicholas Ridley (as Ridley reports) that power was the name of the game, he was usefully reminding us that political motivations have changed little since Machiavelli observed them and shocked rulers by writing them down, and that we ignore such candour at our peril. We need not be so severe as Acton, and we can assume that power may be well used or badly used as we examine it in the context of current European development.

2

Enlargement of the European Union, challenge and chance – an Austrian Perspective

Dr Erhard Busek, 2000.

Dr Erhard Busek is Vice-Chancellor of Austria, Co-ordinator of South-Eastern Europe Co-operative Initiative and former Chairman of the Austrian People's Party.

ENLARGEMENT is the greatest challenge for Europe in the years ahead. Our shared European identity is something that is all too easily taken for granted even in the present EU Member States. To make the best of our common European identity we have to continue to engage with the rest of Europe, we have to identify and seize the opportunities that Europe presents, and we together have to shape Europe in this new twenty-first century. We have to acknowledge and identify ourselves as fellow Europeans.

The key to that future is enlargement. The enlargement of the European Union towards the Central and Eastern European Countries (CEECs) represents an historic process which will help overcome the artificial separation of the continent. The area of stability, welfare and safety that was achieved by European cooperation after the devastating experience of the Second World War can now be expanded towards the East.

As Austria is situated in the heart of Europe, the continental dimension of the European model of a free and voluntary combination of free nations is of particular importance. Our country is moving more towards the centre, politically, economically and strategically. The Austrian government therefore wants to see the EU being enlarged rapidly, successfully. We want to see new members take on and implement the EU's body of laws and practices, to operate as fully-functioning members of the Single Market from day one.

But I am delighted that both they and we are in a position to take it seriously, work at it and further take forward the historic changes seen in our continent in the past decade. Obviously, in many of those countries which are now negotiating their entry to the EU there have already been momentous changes, including in the ways that governments relate to their citizens, and those citizens relate to each other.

Since 1989 we have witnessed profound social and political changes. The fall of the Berlin Wall in 1989 changed the politics of Europe, opening space for a Europe of the future. It meant the end of unnecessary, enforced divisions between national governments, between regional authorities, between towns, and between individuals. And it ended the exclusion of so many members of the European family of nations from the process of European development. Membership of the EU will rebuild the European family, because the EU is precisely about those relationships, at all levels, which are so vital to political, economic, cultural, and social growth and development.

Enlargement will extend the benefits of the single market to all of the new Member States, ensuring a level playing field for all participants. Economic transition has been difficult for the prospective Member States, there is no question of that. And together we have to make sure that when they do join, their economies are ready to withstand the pressures that competition in the single market will bring. But once that is done, there is no doubt that bringing in such dynamic economies, with so many resources and so much enthusiasm to offer, will benefit both old and new Member States.

Austrian industry has already concentrated heavily on the Eastern markets. In the area of foreign trade, Austria could considerably strengthen the positive balance it has obtained from business with the candidate countries from Eastern Europe since the opening of these states: e.g. the balance of trade surplus in 1999 equalled ATS +30 billion in comparison to ATS +7.4 billion in 1989. This represents the highest positive balance for Austria's exports in comparison to certain world regions. Between 1989 and 1999 Austria's exports to Hungary, the Czech Republic, Slovakia and Poland increased more than fourfold while imports only doubled. The CEEC's share of Austrian exports increased from 4.4 per cent in 1989 to 16 per cent in 1999.

Therefore, in relation to the Austrian economy, the Central and Eastern European Countries, especially the candidates of the first enlargement round, represent one of its most important markets outside of the EU, carrying with them economic welfare and the security of work places in our country. Measuring its share of the market Central and Eastern Europe is at the top of the Austrian balance of foreign trade. Of the export market that the Western industrial countries have in the East, our share amounts to 17 per cent in Hungary, 14 per cent in Slovakia, 13 per cent in Slovenia and 9 per cent in the Czech Republic. Compare these figures to our share in Germany, 6.4 per cent, in Italy 3.5 per cent and in the EU as a whole, 2.4 per cent, and it is very clear that Austria's economy profits from the growth of the candidate countries.

Since the opening up of the Eastern European markets Austrian firms have also held a very good position in the area of direct investment. Up to 1998 Austrian enterprises invested 7 billion USD in Eastern European countries totalling a market share of 9 per cent of existing investment capital. This has led to the establishment of approximately 14,000 Austrian subsidiaries and joint ventures in this area. In some countries like Hungary, Slovenia and Slovakia, Austria is one of the main foreign investors. This capital is insured and can carry interest only when the economic situation in the Eastern markets remains stable and shows further signs of development. It will be a considerable contribution to the entry of these countries into the EU.

With the increasing pressure of competition, the attractiveness of Austria's industrial location will depend particularly on the optimal use of cross border cooperation. This use of the optimal mix of locations can make a significant contribution to the improvement of the competitiveness of industry.

The main growth potential of the candidate countries (the growth forecasts of the first five candidates are above the EU average) promises further opportunities for Austria's export industry. It is expected that the inclusion of the CEECs in the single market will accelerate the growth rate of this region and increase its purchasing power. If Austrian products can hold on to their share of the market, it will bring a considerable improvement to the Austrian balance of trade and current account balance.

The additional options for financing the enlargement both before and after accession, made possible by structural funds, will bring new opportunities for European industry. The strengthening of East European infrastructure particularly in the transport, energy and environmental sectors should give rise to more business opportunities.

But enlargement is not just about economics. Enlargement is the only right and sensible response to the changing pressures and circumstances of the past decade and the new century. Enlargement will cement the sense of stability, the respect for democracy, the promotion of human rights and cultural diversity which candidate countries have themselves worked so hard for. These are issues and values that cut across national boundaries, issues that need us to co-operate with and talk to each other. Similarly, there are issues on which we need to take action together, where the European Union is uniquely well placed to provide common solutions, implemented by national governments. As well as the profound political shock brought about by the fall of Communism, the last decade has also seen a revolution in the ways that we think about social and economic policy. The EU is a forum for us to explore, to share and to promote that thinking.

And enlargement is a way for us to extend that process. The countries of Central and Eastern Europe have already made great strides in the policy areas that crucially affect all our citizens' lives. The Commission's latest progress reports on the applicants for membership, issued in October last year, showed how far they have come in a short space of time. But there is still work to be done, and significant investments to be made, both financially and in terms of government time and effort. We all need to prepare well for enlargement.

When taking on a project of this dimension there are bound to be a number of risks involved. There are fears of added strain on the job market, danger along the border areas, disadvantages for agriculture and excessive financial demands.

These anxieties are not to be dismissed but one must also avoid exaggerated horror scenarios. I am convinced that all problems could be coped with once the necessary precautions are taken by the EU and by the candidate countries themselves. The institutions of the EU, as well as the member states, show responsible and planned involvement with the enlargement project. As a result, the Council of the EU heads of state and governments agreed that the accession agreements would come into effect once the internal EU requirements have been met. These include reforms of the agricultural and structural policies, management of public finances and decision making procedures.

In Austria a special attention has been given to the problems of migration and border regions.

Econometric studies from the late 1990s have shown that the number of people willing to migrate from four of the candidate countries, namely from the Czech Republic, Slovakia, Poland and Hungary to the EU totals 700,000. Of those would-be migrants, 150,000 have indicated that Austria would be their preferred target country. It has been estimated that as far as Austria is concerned yearly migration flows would amount to 23,000-40,000 people from the day of accession of the CEECs to the EU. These estimates are all based on figures from the late 1990s; their relevance, though, for projections for the first two decades of this century is basically undisputed. Other factors such as the tightening of migration policies of the EU member states from the early/mid 1990s onwards, the unique geographical location of Austria as well as Austria's strong cultural and historical ties with the neighbouring CEECs, and the fact that most "transition economies" are still unsettled, add a great momentum of uncertainty to any forecasts.

As regards "commuting potential" the situation is even more difficult and unpredictable. As stated, there are very large nominal earnings gaps between Austria and CEEC border regions (at times of the order 15-25:100) There are important uncertainties as to the extent to which the discrepancy between current real income and nominal earnings gaps might be closed over the coming decade. Furthermore, the geographic closeness of large conurbations on both sides of the current Austrian-CEEC borders provide a specific example. Existing estimates of the commuting potential between Austria and its CEE neighbours (between 50,000-70,000 over the first five years after liberalisation with some estimates going up to 150,000 over a ten year period) apply a similar framework to that used for estimating the migration potential. Important explanatory variables are left out of existing studies such as the dependence of commuting on traffic infrastructure and conditions with respect to housing (for weekly, monthly or seasonal commuters). Given the uncertainty surrounding the quantitative potential of migration and commuting flows in the case of full liberalisation of labour market access between Austria and the CEE candidate countries, there is a case for maintaining some type of regulatory framework so that adjustment processes initiated by such liberalisation can be phased in over a certain time horizon.

But we are also playing our part in helping the candidate countries to prepare themselves for enlargement. I am glad to say that our bilateral relations with all of the candidates are excellent. EU programmes mean that over 830,000 young people from across the EU have studied, trained or worked in another Member State. This is building the agenda for the next generation so they are not afraid to say "we are European". And when people's working lives have finished, they can choose to retire and draw their pensions anywhere in the EU. Travel between current Member States is already enriching the lives of millions of people.

I am confident that enlargement will increase travel between the old and new Member States of the EU. The prospect of enlargement is already doing so. Enlargement can only increase the traffic in both directions and by doing so through personal connections, it will finally bring Europe together. The foundations for co-operation were laid by the revolt against Communist rule in Central Europe. It is up to all of us now to build on that co-operation. We have the tools: the EU and the candidate countries have a wealth of resources to offer each other – human, financial, knowledge-based and physical. Successive European Councils have set out the path which both sides must follow towards wider membership. The benefits are clear, and the obligations too.

Our government is working hard towards the common goal of enlargement, and our people are beginning to see the rewards on offer. A step on the way – not an end point.

3

Political Union in Europe

Ronald Butt, 1990.

Ronald Butt is an historian of the British Constitution and was a leader writer for **The Times.**

DESPITE Mrs. Thatcher's hostility to political union in the European Community, she formally agreed at the June summit in Dublin to the convening in December of a Conference on the question alongside the similar conference on economic union in Rome which had already been arranged. The British change of stance was, however, no surprise. It had become clear at the April meeting that Mrs. Thatcher had given way to the insistence of the Foreign Secretary, Mr. Douglas Hurd, that it would be a blunder for her to persist in refusing to talk on the argument that the political union was too impractical to be worth talking about. Mr. Hurd's view was that a refusal to talk would simply mean becoming bogged down in a sterile and protracted procedural row in which Britain would be outnumbered and was bound to be ultimately defeated by the other member states.

That was a correct analysis. It is important to recognise that in the recent strengthening demand for some kind of political

15

union, it has not been M. Jacques Delors, the President of the Commission, who has been making the running but the majority of the other member governments – most conspicuously the French and the Germans. Both of these have done so for their own very different reasons – the French because they want some kind of surety that the Germans will be bound into the Community by whatever institutional means can be devised to ensure that they do not become footloose in the centre of Europe; the Germans because of their anxiety to reassure the French and because their own institutions have made them federally inclined.

Yet neither France nor Germany has any clear notions about the form political union should take: the Germans because they are much too preoccupied with the problems posed by their own reunification to spare time for planning European political union; the French because they are quite well aware that their own sense of nationalism is far too strong for it to be easy for them to find ways and means. Even M. Delors himself has come to accept this as a present fact of life. The French do not, it is true, share the British concern at the idea that the national parliament, so much more central to public life here than in France, could be over-ridden. But the French sense of national sovereignty and identity is at least as strong and deep as the British (if not more so) and there can hardly be any Frenchman who is seduced by the idea of a United States of Europe on the American pattern. They know that this is simply unrealistic.

European Political Union in any clear institutional sense is, therefore, a kind of day-dream, even for its most passionate advocates among the major nations of Europe. (It is rather different for some of the minor countries, notably Belgium, for which it could be a solution to the internal tension between Flanders and Wallonia). Nevertheless, day-dream or inspired vision, there was no way in which France, Germany, Italy and others could be dissuaded from talking about it. In terms of sentiment, the once war-torn countries on the western European mainland feel much more acutely than we do the danger in the attachment to national frontiers. In terms of immediate practical politics, they are also very serious about moving on from the Exchange Rate Mechanism of the European Monetary System to some kind of deeper monetary union and they accept that this raises questions of what kind of political responsibility there should be for a central European bank and a single European currency.

Moreover, they are (as all democrats should be) genuinely concerned about the 'democratic deficit' which has been built up in Brussels. They are anxious about the way in which, by creeping federalism, the bureaucracy there has obtained increasing power over decisions which affect the lives of ordinary people. There is a growing wish in the chanceries of Europe that parliamentary ways should be found of calling Brussels to account and, of course, the remedy which automatically occurs to them is that it should be done by strengthening the powers of the European Parliament – which, equally naturally, is also the remedy which occurs to power-hungry MEPs. The other European governments also brood over the possibility of some kind of European political cabinet in Brussels.

All this may not be very realistic but such is the strength of the French and German determination to have political union on the agenda that it was only good sense for the British to agree to talk about it. Besides, they have now realised that the very vagueness of the French and German positions enables them to do so with impunity.

In advance of Dublin, Mr. Hurd produced some propositions for discussion in the Overseas and Defence Committee of the Cabinet which began to make the general direction of British thinking pretty clear. First, the Government has virtually decided that the European Parliament should not be given the greater powers over Community legislation for which it longs, though the agenda now agreed includes negotiations on the possibility of extending the European Parliament's amending powers.

Instead, the British believe that, following the example of the British House of Commons' Public Accounts Committee and its departmental Select Committees, the European Parliament should seek to define and enhance its powers to investigate the way in which the Brussels executive is operating – and in particular, how well or ill money is spent. It is argued that the House of Commons in England built up its authority through the power of the purse and that the European Parliament should attempt the same. (In fact, the analogy does not altogether serve the argument. Important though the Commons' surveillance of the proper use of appropriated funds has been, their power has, of course, been built on their exclusive right to give or refuse taxation, and to withhold the supply of money on which government depends. This, however, is a separate and a rather academic point. Even the federalists do not yet seem committed outright to the power of the European Parliament to raise taxes over the heads of the national Parliaments.)

There is certainly good sense in the British argument that the European Parliament should focus more on the manner in which money is spent. There are better ways of influencing the Brussels executive than by rushing to give powers to a supra-national Parliament, which would only exacerbate the national resentments which are potentially the Community's greatest danger. For that reason, the British Government would also like to see co-operation between national Parliaments to devise more or less common procedures of investigation and inquiry; and it has looked with a benevolent and approving eye on a recent exploratory meeting between the chairman of the Scrutiny Committee of the House of Commons and his approximate equivalents in other national parliaments. The British government is, however, sceptical about the current fashion of constitution building which preoccupies not only the federalists but also those who describe themselves as 'confederalists'. It therefore seems unlikely that the recent paper produced for the Bruges Group by Dr. Alan Sked of the London School of Economics will have been regarded by British Ministers as having practical possibilities. Accepting the value of the Community economically (save for its notorious Common Agricultural Policy), the benefits of the single market and the contributions of the Community to European peace, Dr. Sked finds it hard to believe that the Community's founding fathers, if they were alive today, 'would be in favour of creating a highly centralised political union, with a powerful central government...dictating economic and social priorities to enfeebled member states.' Nor does he think they would approve of 'recent demands that the vast majority of policy decisions should emanate from Brussels'. Besides, it is Dr. Sked's opinion that the democratisation of eastern European countries will mean that they will 'soon' have the right to participate in some future union, which means that it would be too big to be under any close central control.

Dr. Sked's own answer is to propose a 'Confederation' which would allow union with diversity. He advocates, first, that direct elections to the European Parliament should be ended and that it should become instead an assembly of representatives from national parliaments, reflecting the composition of each domestic legislature. A majority of each national delegation would have the veto on the application to its own country of any legislation of which it disapproved. Dr. Sked is also willing for the European Parliament to have more powers over the European budget and for all Community leglisation to require its approval.

If we were starting from scratch, the idea of integrating the national and European parliaments in this way might seem an attractive one. But it hardly seems practical now. For one thing, there would be the fervent hostility of the directly elected

MEPs (they are now no mean lobby) for whom a new Parliament building is already being constructed in the guise of a conference centre hard by the Community headquarters in Brussels. Their influence in the capitals of the Community is such that they would win their battle. In any case, the idea of an integrated membership of the Community and the national parliaments is probably impractical. If the delegate-MEPs were also MPs of the national parliaments they would kill themselves from overwork, though they could be members of a second national chamber. If, on the other hand they were external nominees, they could seriously detract from the principle of direct election on which the power of national parliaments is rightly based.

At the stage the Community has now reached it would perhaps be easier to adopt Dr. Sked's proposal of a European Cabinet, permanently resident in Brussels, each member of which would have Cabinet status in his national government. His European Cabinet would be responsible for proposing and agreeing European legislation (the Commission would lose its political aspects and have a purely civil service role) and would have an annually rotating president. The existing Council of heads of government would continue, would have responsibility for defence and foreign policy, would vote by the principle of unanimity (except where it was otherwise specifically provided) and could propose legislation itself. Even this, however, goes well beyond what the British government regards as practical.

Though there is much good theoretical sense in Dr. Sked's general argument, its details do not consort easily with the prevailing facts. His assumption that almost all Europe could participate flies in the face of the historical disparity of wealth between east and west Europe which long antedates Communism and, indeed, goes back through the whole of this century. The obligations to provide regional subsidies would provide insuperable problems. His argument also assumes too glibly that the opposing camp of 'federalists' is solely motivated by a hankering after centralisation when there are many in Brussels who argue rather that it is because bureaucratic federalism has *already* come into existence that we must now find workable means to control it politically. In many respects, the British 'federalists' of the Bexley variety over-state their case (almost as though national feeling hardly mattered) in a way that the more realistic federalists do not. In Brussels there is much more concern to accept that national accountability matters and must be provided for.

A concern to delineate more clearly what should be the responsibility of the Community and what should be reserved to the nation states is also the basis of Mr. Hurd's thinking and in effect Mrs. Thatcher has now adopted something like the same position. In other words, the British, though from a rather different stance, have adopted a version of the doctrine of 'subsidiarity' which has hitherto been the language of the federalists. There is at least this much common ground: the agenda now agreed for the Rome conference specifically acknowledges that nothing should be done at Community level except those things which are best done there – though there are vast differences of opinion about what precisely this should mean.

It is this concept of subsidiarity that underlies the challenge which the Prime Minister (now that she has agreed to discuss the concept of political union) has issued to the other member governments: she has asked them to say what, in their various views, should be definitely excluded from the Community's powers. The answer of the British government itself is to start with the exclusion of the authority of national parliaments, systems of law and decisions on war and peace. Yet it is important to note that, in respect of the evolution of foreign and defence policy on which the decisions of peace and war hang, the British government stands in a position which some may find surprisingly Community-minded.

Arguing that Britain has always been in the forefront of European foreign policy co-operation, the Government insists that it is prepared to go further in reaching common positions on such questions as international security, disarmament, the implementation of the Helsinki act and so on. Sir Leon Brittan, the Vice-President of the Commission has recently gone further still. He has advocated the creation of a European Security Community (alongside the EC), which would formulate its own collective defence policy and require greater integration of forces, thus providing a specifically European pillar within NATO. Quite apart from the eventual possibility thus opened up of a European nuclear deterrent and common research and development, it would imply a very considerable degree of *common* foreign policy – and thus, in a pragmatic sort of way, of pooled sovereignty.

It might be assumed that Mrs. Thatcher, with her stress on sovereign states, would personally be hostile to this sort of approach. Yet it is worthwhile to recall that she herself, early in her Prime Ministership and long before her celebrated Bruges speech, advocated greater contact between the EC and NATO which, though they inhabited the same city, had no formal contact. (At the time, I recall, she was jeered at by Community enthusiasts for being ignorant of the fact that the EC was not that sort of body and that such contact was out of the question.) Though Sir Leon's approach goes well beyond the Government's current thinking, it is possible that she sees some possibility of common ground in it. At all events, it does not seem that Mr Hurd wishes instantly to shoot it right out of the sky.

There seems to be only one substantial difference of principle between Sir Leon's approach and Mr. Hurd's undisguised belief that the way ahead lies with increasing the already existing practice by which the Community arrives at common foreign policy decisions after initiatives have been taken by one or another of the member governments. That difference lies in the fact that the shared foreign policy decisions taken at present are largely responses (whether at the official level or through the Council of Ministers) to events as and when they arise. The sort of foreign and defence policy co-operation implicit in Sir Leon's approach would seem clearly to require eventually a *constant* collectivity, much as exists in a Cabinet, which would attempt preparations in anticipation of the future. Looked at in one way, this is only a change of degree; looked at in another, it is a change in kind.

The important question is how far a more integrated foreign and defence policy would require new political institutions of a supra-national kind and how far it could be managed on the basis of a constant 'confederal' council of independent sovereign states. The same, of course, applies to economic policy and especially to any agreed monetary union beyond the exchange rate mechanism. What would be the political implications of a free-standing central bank (*Bundesbank*-style) and of a single currency? On both foreign and economic policy, British ministers are clearly prepared for greater co-operation, just as they do not blink at the role of the Community in such matters as the environment, trade and (little though they love the CAP) agriculture.

The stumbling block for the British is the building of federalist institutions which would alienate national sovereignty, over-ride Parliament and bring supranational intervention to bear on matters which nations should decide for themselves. The government believes that the other member states, for all their fervent talk of federalism, will find that in practice they agree with the British about this more than they themselves have yet understood. The British approach to political unity by way of greater pragmatic co-operation between the governments of the member states and the member parliaments may well prove to be a better way forward than by new institution-building.

What the British are doing is to call the others' bluff on political union. At the preliminary discussion at Dublin in

May, when the question was discussed, there were already some signs that they had judged right. It was a reflection of a more pragmatic mood that M. Delors should have been quoted as saying: 'We cannot reach even a minimum of consensus if we talk now of the *final* vision of political union' (my italics). Still more to the point was the admission of the French Foreign Minister, M. Roland Dumas that 'no country is ready in 1990 to give up sovereignty over foreign and security matters.' That, of course, is no more than everyone already knew about French attitudes and the only question is how much policy affecting each nation's internal affairs also realistically comes into that category. In practice, I would guess that there is much more of it than the French, Germans, Italians and Belgians are as yet willing to admit. It is not, after all, solely in the higher atmosphere of foreign affairs that things happen which most closely engage the national interests and sentiments of individual countries. Mrs. Thatcher's defence of national sovereignty and institutions potentially covers much of these as well.

That, however, does not mean that the members of the Community should not draw more closely together in political terms. On the contrary, the less tension there is over frustrated national interests, the closer the member nations will be prepared to be to each other. By pushing the other Community countries to analyse and say what they mean when they speak of political union without defining it, the British Government has taken the right path. The British are also right to take part themselves in the process by which each government will present its own more detailed ideas of how political union should be approached and what institutional change is needed. The British Government has nothing to lose and everything to gain by talking and Mr. Douglas Hurd is to be congratulated for having made sure that it did. In the Community, there are sometimes issues over which confrontation is unavoidable but talking about European political unity is not one of them.

4

Safeguarding the British Constitution

Ronald Butt, 1990.

THE British people have good cause to guard their constitution. In its evolution it has served the cause of liberty well for at least eight centuries. Its characteristics are its roots in precedent, its unbroken continuity and its normal classification as 'unwritten'. In fact, of course, a great deal of what is essential to it was written down, from Magna Carta to the Bill of Rights, the Act of Settlement and the enactments which have established the franchise and limited the power of the House of Lords. What we mean by unwritten is that there is no rounding document, no attempt to entrench detailed prescriptions which, embodying the specific ideas of a particular time, are likely to be unsuitable for application in some unforeseeable future circumstances, at least without amendment. We have never had a statement of general principles and formal constitutional provision such as the Americans have. Nor have we ever had the kind of constitutions that (as in France for instance) are written to establish a form of government for one regime, only to be torn up and replaced by another rounding document to establish its successor. The concept of a 'regime' is one wholly alien to the British approach to government, which is rooted in pragmatic continuity.

The profound importance of this attitude to government lies in its implicit recognition that, human nature being what it is, it is fruitless to try to arrange government by expressing absolute principles and then trying to apply them by means of immutable constitutional arrangements. Circumstances change in ways we cannot anticipate; that is why even written constitutions which survive (as in America) cannot do so without amendment. At every stage since Magna Carta, therefore, the unwritten British constitution has been expressed in concrete terms, by means of particular enactments for the redress of particular grievances and for the guarantee of specific liberties. These enactments, however, also symbolise and express more general principles. There is an instinctive understanding that, behind each remedy for a particular abuse, general principles exist which are too large to be constrained by what can be expressed through the limited understanding of any one age.

The specific provisions have, therefore, to be adjusted from time to time so that they represent the underlying philosophical concepts of equity and justice in a form that best represents new needs. Parliamentary government is the means of doing so. Beneath the apparent vagueness of the British approach to constitutional principle and the fluidity of British political practice, one fundamental principle has prevailed at almost every stage in English affairs since the Anglo-Saxons settled the land. It is that government should be conducted by consent and that the executive power should govern and legislate by consultation with the representatives of the community (whether or not they were elected) to discover what was needed and what acts of government were likely to be generally acceptable. Since at least the 14th century it has been assumed that this consultation should take place through a Parliament with an elected element. Since the end of the 17th century the sanction of that elected element has been fundamental to the survival of any government and its policies.

This principle now stands in jeopardy as a result of the piecemeal way in which the determination of our affairs is being absorbed into the governance of the European Community with its lack of 'responsible' (in the technical sense) government. Ironically, our very very reluctance to rely on written constitutions and our dislike of constitutional blueprints makes us more vulnerable to the erosion of our political liberties by easy unresisted stages.

To recognise the danger is not an expression of anti-Community sentiments; it is not to revive the old 'anti-Market' campaign. There is an overwhelming balance of advantage on the side of our combination with other Western European states in the Community, not only on economic but also on political and (at some future date) on defence matters. It is necessary not only to maintain the internal cohesion of Western Europe which has made war among its states unthinkable but also to lessen a dependence on the United States which could come to rest on conditions that we might allow ourselves to regard as unacceptable if we were free to pursue our own European destiny. What is at issue for Britain is not our membership of the Community but the political nature of the organisation to which, in the future, we freely consent to be a party.

Of course, the informed public hears from time to time of the inability of Westminster to exert any real control over the Community directives which pass through parliament on the nod; it hears of what seem to be the absurdly bureaucratic and jargonised interventionism of the Community. But such is the mire of unintelligible detail that it seems in practice that there is nothing to be done about it. The easiest course is to trust to the government, acting through the Council of Ministers, to defend our interest on those things that really are central. We may feel further reassured by Mrs. Thatcher's clear insistence, not only in her Bruges speech but long before, on the preservation of British sovereignty. It is easy to overlook the fact that she will not be in Downing Street for ever, and that in any case politicians can change their tune when necessity presses.

Above all, the major issues are not put to the electorate in terms of clear questions requiring clear answers, yet we are accustomed to think politically by responding to questions requiring the answer 'yes' or 'no' and in default of having these questions put to it, the public has no means of reaching an informed and thought-out position. Unfortunately when the British electorate votes in the forthcoming European elections it will not be asked, by any side, to give a verdict, even of a provisional kind, on any of the substantial questions concerning our relationship to the Community. The voting will be related almost entirely to political attitudes on domestic politics. We shall be invited to vote in the light of our opinion of Mrs. Thatcher's performance at home or in wider international affairs, the credibility of Mr. Kinnock and the Labour Party to provide an alternative government, and on whether we wish to promote the political centre parties.

The issue that is really relevant to these elections, however, is very different. Mrs. Thatcher has forcefully stated that in the Europe of the single market, the place for national sovereignty and democracy must be preserved and it might be supposed that, since no propositions exist for any alternative arrangement to provide for democratically responsible Community power, her argument was simply a statement of the obvious. Indeed, her opponents find it convenient to interpret it as nothing more than a manifestation of gratuitous dislike for the Community. Yet the very hostility that her statement has attracted from the Euro-fanatics and the aficionados of Brussels, is a sign that she has touched a sensitive nerve. The scathing and patronising scorn poured on Mrs. Thatcher's attitude by such public figures as Lord Cockfield, Lord Jenkins of Hillhead and Mr. Edward Heath (which revives the memory of the rage of many of them when, in the pre-Fontainebleau negotiations about Britain's budgetary contributions, she was accused of referring to 'our' money as though that were an intolerably vulgar concept) informs us, not about her position, but about theirs.

Their position is, of course, a kind of de facto federalism which is not openly presented as such but is revealed by their bitter hostility to anyone who even raises the question whether a drift towards federalism is in prospect. The truth is that they do not wish the matter to be discussed. For myself, I pay M. Delors the compliment of believing that when he spoke of the prospect that in ten years time 80 per cent of the economic decisions of the whole Community would be taken in Brussels, he meant precisely what he said. Assuming that he did, it has the most serious implications for the kind of democratic responsibility we have nurtured (and, indeed, for that of other member states). For clearly, in practice, those decisions will be formulated by the Commission. Nor does he specify the nature of the 20 per cent of decisions which he implies will *not be* made in Brussels. Will these decisions be of major importance or minor?

The prediction of M. Delors, of course, matches closely Lord Cockfield's advocacy of a 'single market' and the belief of many other politicians in complete integration. It must follow that a single economy and the taking of most major decisions centrally would only be possible through the power of what would be tantamount to a central authority or government – in other words by what would virtually be a 'federal' administration.

To say this is not automatically to condemn such a state of affairs. It is merely to emphasize that if this is to be the future then we must go towards it with our eyes open, knowing what is in store, freely accepting it and knowing how to provide for it adequately in institutional terms. For myself, there are some respects in which I could personally feel a degree of attraction towards the European federal idea – but only in certain circumstances that are now probably unattainable. If it had been possible to apply confederalist principle to the original six member countries (Charlemagne's empire) plus Britain, if it could be duly equipped with appropriate representative democratic institutions, if there were entrenched national rights for individual states and if there were a 'federal' parliament able to call the 'federal' government to account, I could see some case for it. Such a compact federation or confederation of states with the advantage of much shared culture could make sense. It would, however, be quite impossible to apply such a system to the far-flung Community which embraces countries from Denmark to Greece and the Iberian peninsula and may spread wider to embrace Turkey. So if such a federal or confederal system is that towards which M. Delors, Lord Cockfield, Lord Jenkins and others wish us move they should say so candidly and explain in detail what proposals they have to make it politically accountable.

But for various reasons they are clearly prepared to do nothing of the sort. The Euro-sophisticates, such as Lord Jenkins, think it vulgar and unsubtle to speak so bluntly. To raise these questions they take as a sign of either ignorance or of the lingering anti-Market national patriotism that they have always so much despised. On the other hand, the Eurotechnocrats (Lord Cockfield, for instance) do not speak of the political dimension because, I suspect, they do not think it greatly matters. For them, trade and the economy, and whatever social change is necessary to promote them, are technical matters to be determined by experts impeded by the least possible interference from a political process resting on the mere wishes and opinions of ordinary people reacting through the ballot box. Least of all should politics get in the way of expertise when they are motivated by anything so prejudiced, not to say irrational, as instincts of national feeling.

But it is not only the club of Euro-fanatics and technocrats who do not wish these matters to be discussed before the people. The Labour Party, for instance, which not long since was locked in xenophobic dislike of the European connection, has now formally (and rightly) accepted that Britain is in the Community to stay. Moreover, it has been instructed by M. Delors that the Community could be an invaluable vehicle for international socialism and for standardised social practices throughout the member states. This alarms some Conservatives. But in their party there is a reluctance to bring the matter into open debate because, if it came to the point, there would be too many uncomfortable divisions among themselves on the matter of the Community's institutional future. Among Tory Euro-MPs, the majority seems to incline towards Mrs. Thatcher's opinion that national sovereignty must have an abiding place in the Community. Nevertheless, the Euro-MPs work in a quasi-federalist culture and amid much quasi-federalist rhetoric. They also no doubt feel that in an integrated (federalist) Europe there would be a much bigger political role for the European Parliament as a check upon Brussels. For one reason or another, therefore, there is little enthusiasm on any side for addressing the constitutional future of Europe.

This is mistaken for two reasons. The first is that, though it has become fashionable to treat 'nationalism' as a dangerous instinct, it is far from being the principal cause of human wars and strife. There were tribal, dynastic, feudal and religious wars long before there were wars motivated by nationalism. War is as likely to be caused by the suppression of nationalism as by its worship and today, as we see most obviously in the Soviet Union, national minorities struggle for the right to govern themselves and to live together as nations. It is quite impossible to believe that the ability of the nations of the Community to express themselves as such could be subordinated to a central authority without some kind of eventual explosion.

It is no answer to insist that the member nations would be in no danger of losing their identity. Indeed, if they could lose it there would be no problem. But they will remain nations and if Scottish nationalism presents problems for the United Kingdom, how much greater would be the problem of British nationalism within the Community if the British felt unrepresented and repressed? To get into a position in which, without due public debate and agreement, nationalism was *de facto* submerged would therefore be highly dangerous. Nothing would be worse than to progress by undebated stages into such a position so that the people did not understand where they were going.

The second and even greater danger is the erosion of parliamentary sovereignty. For the present, we depend on the British presence on the Council of Ministers to safeguard the national interest since Westminster is plainly unequipped to do so. There is no way in which the British Members of the European Parliament could ever fulfil this role, even if that Parliament had more power over Brussels and over the Council of Ministers. For in the European Parliament each nation is (as such) in a permanent minority. Each *national* majority can be over-ridden by the international majority. Nor can the representatives of any nation on the Council of Ministers be permanently relied on to defend that interest adequately as the majority voting rule gradually erodes the ability of any individual to exercise a veto through a requirement of unanimity.

It is against this background that we should consider the implications of the demand for a central currency and bank and the transfer of their functions to the Community, which Lord Cockfield seems to think will remedy the mistakes of national finance ministers. (He apparently believes that at this higher level ministers and functionaries will be spared the human error to which national politicians are prone and will more easily make decisions of platonic perfection.) The reality, however, is that a single European currency will eventually mean a sole European currency, which would require some kind of quasi-federal political body to control it. On this analysis, there is hardly any aspect of social and economic policy which would be really autonomous and no basic decisions would be taken by a government that was responsible to a properly representative parliament.

For a European Parliament elected on universal suffrage across frontiers could not in practice be elected on a clear European platform in such a way that the majority in each country cast its votes understanding as clearly as it does in a national election what the consequences of that vote might be. What is at issue is nothing less than both national and responsible government. That is why we must not be denied open public debate. (The demand for a Bill of Rights, fashionable with many fervent supporters of Community power, is no answer. Responsible government is not helped by broad and vague statements of principle which are then left to judges, instead of the people's elected representatives, to express in concrete form).

Part of the answer could lie in some parliamentary mechanism, perhaps a second Chamber of Nationalities in the European Parliament, through which national reservations can be expressed effectively. Second, if there is to be a degree of confederalism is must be based on a properly elected political centre responsible to the Community Parliament. The bureaucratic Commission is not enough. Finally, Westminster must have its rights entrenched so that they cannot be over-ridden. The nation states of Europe must not continue to be downgraded by stealth. How precisely this is to be avoided is not easy to see but it would at least be a step towards the answers if we openly discussed the questions. There must be debate.

5

A 19th Century View of Europe – Is it still the same?

John Coleman, 1991.

John Coleman is Editor of **New European** *and the author of various books, including* **Coleman's Drive***.*

THE controversial historian, James Anthony Froude, saw the scene in continental Europe as a dangerous balance of power game which England would only inflame more by meddling in it. I want to illustrate this in this article with some fragments from his diaries and other writings and then ask the question whether the European Economic Community, the European Community and now the European Union is not in reality a continuation of the balance of power politics which evolved on the continent since the fall of the Roman Empire, but within the circumscribed context of a union which has the advantage, admittedly a very big one, of being economic rather than military.

Around the middle of the 19th century Froude wrote:

> I regarded the Reformation as the grandest achievement of English history, yet it was equally obvious that it could never have been brought about constitutionally according to modern methods. The Reformation had been the work of two powerful

sovereigns, Henry VIII and Elizabeth, backed by the strongest and bravest of their subjects. To the last up to the defeat of the Armada, manhood suffrage in England would at any moment have brought back the Pope.

Thus I thought Carlyle was right, and more than ever attached myself to him. He had endless worshippers. A thousand voices, as he said to me, told him he was a great man. But scarce one was a disciple, scarce one would do what he bade them do. I, for my solitary part, believed in him, and in all that I thought or attempted I allowed his judgement to guide me. Thus I was no more enthusiastic than he about the great Exhibition [of 1851], and cared as little for what was called progress and the glorification of liberty. Liberty, as I understood it, meant the freedom which a man wins when he is master of his trade, the freedom which he wins as a moral being when he has conquered his lower nature, is no longer led astray by passion or inferior motive, but can stand amidst temptation by his own strength, can govern himself and so is fit to direct others. The liberty which means emancipation from restraint, the liberty which will leave the young and the old, the wise and the foolish, the worthless and the worthy alike, free to do as they please and have an equal voice in the commonwealth, appeared then to me and appears now a delusion, and the demand for it to be one of those epidemics of passion which at various periods have swept over the human race: an epidemic like that of the Crusades, which appears while it lasts to be the holiest and noblest of causes, and is looked back upon when over as insanity. The Crusades fever lasted two hundred years and cost Europe six million lives. The Revolutionary Liberty fever will perhaps last as long and cost as much more.

There is an irony in nature which corrects, even while the fever is on, the extremity of extravagance. The Prince's Exhibition was to have inaugurated an era of universal peace. Within two years of its close we were launched into the Crimean War. It was not a beautiful thing to see: a Crusade reversed, but, like the others, farmed by popular enthusiasm. The newspapers ordered it. The politicians, afraid for their seats, spoke and voted as they were required. Lord Palmerston provided a watchword. He dared to say that it was a war of civilization against barbarism; the Turk representing civilization and the Russians the other thing. Lies are costly when believed in.

At the bottom, perhaps, the true cause of the business was the ambition of certain European statesmen to make a United Germany an ambition which could not be realized unless the strength of Russia was for a time paralysed. France and England were made cat's paws to take the chestnuts out of the fire. The result was something. It freed Italy. It did enable Germany to become a great nation. It cost Russia 200,000 lives and gave the Ottomans a renewal of their lease of existence for another quarter or half century. England spent eighty millions of money, sacrificed a hundred thousand brave men, exhibited an administrative incompetence which realized absurdly Carlyle's description of Downing Street, obtained a certain amount of imaginary glory and real discredit. England, France, Italy, and Turkey, with Austria neutral, had succeeded at last in wresting from Russia half a single town and a treaty which was soon torn to pieces. Our reputation as a military power fell under a cloud, and the Crimean War was followed almost immediately by the Indian Mutiny.

Events in India were in singular contrast with the incapacity which had degraded the Crimean administration. The English nature had not degenerated. Englishmen high and low are the same men who won our Eastern empire under Clive and Hastings. A mere handful of English soldiers and civilians – surprised, divided, scattered over the face of the enormous peninsula, decimated by treachery and massacre – faced in the field the native army which they had drilled, defeated them, stormed their fortified cities, delicate ladies facing shot and steel as coolly as their husbands, and by the rapidity, the completeness, and stern resolution with which they crushed the universal revolt taught the world to know that the blunders at Sebastopol were no measure of the English strength. India had been spared the invasion of constitutionalism, and British India statesmen and generals were free to use both brain and hand.

In great extremities the eloquent tongues fall silent. The heart of the nation is in its armies. Constitutional anarchy would have ruined Rome. French soldiers saved the credit of the Revolution. The sword of Cromwell had to rescue the cause of the Civil Wars from the weak generosity of the Long Parliament. The rule of a democracy, said a Roman historian, is bad by necessity, for it depends on the votes of the majority, and the majority of men are always fools, while the gods did occasionally set the single wise man at the head of things. The suppression of the Mutiny gladdened the heart and kindled the spirit of every Englishman who was proud of his country.

Froude clearly believed in patriotism but absolutely not in that form of nationalism that believes in subduing others, imperialism in the aggressive sense. As he said in a letter to Lady Derby in 1880, when Disraeli's Conservatives had been routed:

I am glad that there is to be an end of 'glory and gunpowder', but my feelings about Gladstone remain what they were. When you came into power in 1874, I dreamed of a revival of real Conservatism which under wiser guiding might and would have lasted to the end of the century. This is gone – gone for ever. The old England of order and rational government is past and will not return. Now I should like to see a moderate triumvirate – Lord Hartington, Lord Granville, and your husband, with a Cabinet which they could control. This too may easily be among the impossibilities, but I am sure that at the bottom of its heart the country wants quiet, and a Liberal revolutionary sensationalism will be just as distasteful to reasonable people as 'Asian Mysteries', tall talk, and ambitious buffooneries.

Waldo Hilary Dunn, Froude's most recent biographer, points out that his reflections on his country's history led him to the same conclusions as George Washington:

Washington left as a legacy to his countrymen a warning never to entangle themselves in European complications. The Americans have remembered the lesson and have acted upon it.

They do not fret themselves into agitation over the 'balance of power'... Inevitably and properly the English colonies will desire to imitate America's example... Therefore it is quite certain that if it be England's intention to adhere to her old pretensions, if England persists that she will be the arbiter of Europe (although on the European continent she owns not an acre, save Gibraltar Rock, and never can acquire an acre), the colonists will wisely decline a nearer union with us. Even now the present light connecting thread lays them open to serious danger. Those who meddle in quarrels in which they have but an artificial interest are likely in the end to make enemies of all who are vitally concerned. It is possible I do not say it is probable – that if England adheres to these courses she may provoke again, as she has done before, a European combination against her as a general nuisance. She may find her supremacy even on her own ocean disputed by the united fleets of injured and resentful powers; ugly visitors may look in upon her undefended colonial harbours; ugly demands may be presented at sea towns like Melbourne, with threats of shell and rocket if they are refused. To these casualties the colonies are liable already. In a political union with us they would have to share the cost of the ambitious elevation which it pleases us to claim – a cost incalculably great, and incurred for objects which prudent men will not think to be worth the outlay. If the colonists are as wise as I believe them to be, they will resolutely refuse to take on themselves any such dangerous obligations. Glory we may gain in these contests; but glory as barren as it will be hardly won... We may sink our enemies' ironclads, we may ruin their commerce, and we may spend in doing it our hundreds of millions which we shall leave posterity to pay. If the English people are so enamoured of their European position that on these conditions they mean to cling to it, they are masters of their own destiny. But let them understand that in choosing this course they will part company with the rest of their kindred. The empire of the New World, the empire of peace and prosperity, they abandon forever. Now in this our own generation we stand at the parting of the ways. Choose whom you will serve – whether the old spirit which you call honour, and which another age may call madness and dishonour; or the spirit which in the fire and cloud led these millions of our brothers out of the Egypt of vain ambition, into the promised land of industry and self respect –

Choose, and your choice shall be
Brief, and yet endless:
briefly made, and endless in its consequences.

To me, English statesmen seem like the man who had a hundred sheep, and left his ninety-nine to stray and forsake him if they pleased, and wandered off after the worst and most scabbed of his flock – after some phantom of prestige, some vapoury image, like that which mocked Ixion. What are Europe and its dissensions to us, that we should heap tax on tax, add ship to ship and battalion to battalion, because a few million souls are to pass from one sovereign to another – because Germany is growing stronger than France, or Russia is gaining ground against the Turks?

The balance of power! Why is the balance of power more to us than to America? If other nations are strong, let us make ourselves strong. But the pretence itself is but an excuse. No other country dreams of meddling with England. Our danger, when it comes, will be, as it always has been, from our own meddling first with others. Let the Great Powers go at it, exhaust their treasuries, take the labourers from the field and the horse from the plough, arm the one with rifle, and yoke the other to the cannon. Let them convert Europe into an arena, where the bears and base dogs shall tear each other for age after age, and where each generation shall follow in the bloody footprints of its predecessor. But let it be understood that we mean, for our part, to be henceforth spectators of these performances, and that we will act in them no more. The Channel marks us off from the Continental stage. The enterprise of our own people has built another for us – a stage where we fear no rivals, and can play in contrast our own drama of peace. If we need allies, let us turn our faces, not eastward to Europe, but westward beyond the Atlantic.

I have said much of the Americans. They are the people of the future. In the Americans we may read the character and tendencies of the ages that are to be. They are sprung, like us, from the loins of our own fathers. They claim an equal share with us in the traditions of English history; and their great men trace their descent with as much pride from historical English families. Theirs, as well as ours, are the Plantagenet and Tudor princes. Theirs are Drake and Raleigh, Burghley and Cromwell. Theirs are Chaucer and Shakespeare and Bunyan. In our modern poets and men of science, in Scott and Byron, in Burns and Tennyson, in Macaulay and Carlyle, in Tyndall, in Huxley, in Darwin, in John Mill, they will allow us no exclusive right of possession. Let any Englishmen, whom the Americans have learnt to respect, go over among them and see if he is received as a stranger. Their voluntary and instinctive sympathies prove that between the American and the English people there are bonds uniting them closer than those which unite any nations on the globe, and only the action of what are called the governing classes among us prevents the political relations from becoming as intimate as the spiritual. An American alliance is worth all French, Australian, German, Italian, Greek, Turk – all European alliances together. We two nations standing back to back, with our separate governments, but one in heart and one in policy, they with their enormous continent, we with a no less vast colonial union, may then spread into an innumerable company of English, Scotch, and Irish born freemen; and, secure in our own deserved prosperity, we may leave Europe to work out its own destiny. Can imagination picture a fairer prospect for us? There would be no risk of war then, for who would have a motive to quarrel with us? Who would dare to quarrel with us? There would be no danger of colonial disintegration, for what colony would dream of leaving so splendid an association? Little need should we then have to boast of the army corps that we can move, or of the number of campaigns that we can bear, or to start in alarm when fools talk of England's prestige being in danger. From the sure and serene heights of power and confidence we could smile at the envy which sneered at England's decadence.

Ninety years ago, when all generous hearts were beating with hope at the opening of the French Revolution, Jean Paul said: 'On the sunset gate of this century stands written, "Here is the way to virtue and wisdom", as at the western gate of Cherson stands the proud inscription, "Here is the way to Byzantium". Infinite Providence, thou wilt cause the day to dawn!' Three generations have gone by, and, for Europe, that day has not dawned. It is still 'the twelfth hour of the night'. The 'birds of prey are still on the wing', and dock and arsenal ring loud as ever with preparations for mutual slaughter. How is it with England? It may please our princes and aristocracies to challenge their parts in this hard and lurid prospect. Kings and emperors and dukes and field marshals are all that they know or care for in the human family. The rest of us fly after the vain glitter of these people as moths fly about a candle. We all feel honoured in paying taxes, and killing and being killed, at these illustrious persons' bidding. I feel honour in nothing of the kind.

Let the 'rest of us' look to ourselves. America saw its way long ago, and cast their lots with their own kindred. There lies the way to our Byzantium – not eastward through the Sea of Marmora, where queen and cabinet are trying to drive us, but far off through the sunset gate which leads into the New World.

In a change of policy, in a disregard forever of a past which is out of date, in the hearty embracing of a new future, when all English-speaking races will have one interest, and English and Americans, Australians, Canadians, South Africans, shall rank side by side for the common good of mankind there, and nowhere else, lies the solution of the colonial problem. Give us that, and we need look no further. The British Empire will be held together by a magnetism which no local or selfish ambition can then decompose. All difficulties will vanish then. No province of such an empire will be denuded of its wealth, denuded of its genius, denuded of its selfdependence, where the life-blood of the heart will flow freely to the furthest extremities. I saw in Natal a colossal fig-tree. It had a central stem, but I knew not where the centre was, for the branches bent to the

42

ground and struck root there; and at each point a fresh trunk shot up erect, and threw out new branches in turn, which again arched and planted themselves, till the single tree had become a forest, and overhead was spread a vast dome of leaves and fruit, which was supported on innumerable columns, like the roof of some vast cathedral. I saw an image, as I looked at it, of the future of England and her colonies, if the English people can read the signs of the times.

Dunn commented:

The future was to be far worse than even Froude foresaw. "I have no hope that things will go right or that men will think reasonably," he wrote in 1885, "till they have first exhausted every possible mode of human folly."

'Perhaps,' wrote Dunn in 1963, 'it is still too early to hope that every possible mode of human folly has been exhausted'.

There are clearly far-reaching implications both for the recent European adventure and for the 'modern constitutional methods' in these extracts. I believe that neither Europe nor any of the other continents of the world will achieve harmony and peace until the principle implied in Froude's image of the fig tree is understood and realised through the characteristic branches of their own civilisations.

An article in *The Times* on 23rd February 2000 by Sir Trevor Lloyd-Hughes, Harold Wilson's Press Secretary and Chief Information Officer to his government asks the question 'Is Blair the New Wilson?' and reveals a surprising side of Wilson's character which shows that little has changed since the events of the days over which Froude agonised:

Harold Wilson, too, a more modest chap than our present Prime Minister, had his Walter Mitty moment over Europe. We were in Bonn for the funeral of Dr Adenauer, the German Chancellor.

Over three days, Wilson buzzed bee-like among the heads of the six EEC countries, the seven European Free Trade Area nations, President Johnson and others. He told me: "This working funeral is the most comprehensive get-together of European leaders since the Congress of Vienna in 1815."

Smarter than Talleyrand, he was running diplomatic rings round them all, even de Gaulle. Jean Monnet, "father" of the Common Market, boosted his euphoria by opining that de Gaulle was opposing our entry into the EEC because he was afraid of yielding to Wilson the political leadership of Europe,

And so, in the embassy garden on the final morning, Harold confided to me: "Trevor, my real, deepest ambition is to become the master of Europe's destiny."

Only Churchill was not in this tradition and perhaps saw the world in its various circles as struggling to achieve the principle of the 'fig tree'. The mistake that Hitler, Napoleon and Heath made, though of course the last by different means, was that they all wanted to create a centralised Europe with one great trunk standing alone. The first two failed. So perhaps will the last.

The principle of the 'fig tree' also underlies the thinking of Leopold Kohr, which is clearly expressed in his great work *The Breakdown of Nations*. But perhaps the last word on the subject should be reserved for the story of Churchill and Stalin at the Yalta Conference. Stalin is reputed to have said to Churchill that after the war only the eagles would count and Churchill retorted that he wanted a world where all the small birds would be able to survive.

References

Waldo Hilary Dunn, *James Anthony Froude: A Biography* (Volumes One and Two) (Oxford: Clarndon Press, 1963)

Sir Trevor Lloyd-Hughes, 'Is Blair the New Wilson?', *The Times*, 23 February 2000

6

Money, Politics and Europe

Ralf Dahrendorf, 1990.

Lord Dahrendorf was Warden of St Antony's College, Oxford. He is former Director of the London School of Economics and has also been a Government Minister in West Germany and a Commissioner of the European Community.

I begin my article with the argument which the late Sir Brandon Rhys Williams put forward in a paper for the European League for Economic Co-operation on 28 October, 1986: 'We must organize our time-zone' (he said there, with an interesting expression which seems to anticipate the now fashionable European Economic Space though, of course, Britain's time-zone is still one hour behind that of continental Europe) 'working together in a joint act of will to make the most of the opportunities lying open to us between Tokyo and New York.' This is not simple; it is, for example, not just a matter of becoming a member of this or that mechanism. He continued:

'For Britain the choice is not whether to join or not to join the EMS while we continue to run our affairs more or less as before: if we do not quickly make a success of our membership of the European Economic Community we shall be unlikely to make a success of anything else. We have allowed the sterling area to disintegrate. Now the pound is neither a large enough currency to compete with the dollar and the yen on level terms, nor small enough to hang on to some other national currency in a subordinate role.'

The obvious conclusion, Brandon Rhys Williams added, is to create 'an increasingly intimate relationship with the financial centres of the continent. I believe that we can, and must. There is no time to waste. In economic affairs, nationalism is not enough.'

Three-and-a-half years later, things have moved on. Rather, they have first moved forward towards the Single European Market with its implications of a common capital market, and further to the Delors Committee report about monetary union, and they have then moved sideways to a new dominant theme of public and political concern, the larger Europe. Let me begin at the topical end, if only because the 'revolution of 1989' which has set our European neighbours east of the now scrapped Iron Curtain free, raises issues of the relationship between economics and politics which have implications and lessons for the process of European integration.

Communism in Eastern Europe was never a stable system. It was imposed from outside, and resisted by the people. The post-war history of the communist countries is marked by the revolts and uprisings of 1953 in East Germany, 1956 in Hungary, 1968 in Czechoslovakia, 1981 in Poland. More recently, two significant changes have released the internal tensions of Eastern Europe. One of these has a name, Mikhail Gorbachev. His 'Sinatra Doctrine' (to quote his press spokesman Gerasimov), according to which all former satellites can 'do it their way', may yet turn out to be the most consequential reform of all. It has led people to go out into the streets and demand democracy first, and now, in 1990, to exercise their new-found rights in elections, and through freely chosen representatives and governments. The other change which led to 1989 was the increasingly unbearable divergence of economic development in West and East. The OECD countries have experienced a second economic miracle, whereas the COMECON countries have actually declined economically in the 1980s. Given the inevitable flow of information, this led to an untenable situation. Things, meaning the powers that be, had to give.

But what is 'their way' for the countries of East Central Europe? Some believe that it is bound to be 'our way', and that the only alternative to communism is capitalism. In one sense, they are right. In any case, the myth of a 'third way' is as misleading as the dogma of the system which solves all problems. The open society, the constitution of liberty, the rule of law are general virtues of life in freedom which do not and cannot recognise a halfway house. But there is another point. East Europeans like to say: 'We have not left the East in order to join the West, but in order to rejoin Europe.' In other words, they have not swapped one system for another one, but have chosen freedom; they have not left one bloc to become part of the other, but to join .the attempt on the part of the small and medium-sized countries of Europe to organise their affairs – our affairs! – more sensibly.

These are ideas which govern both political and economic reform in the post-communist world. Their immediate relevance in the present context is that we, the more fortunate Europeans, must always bear in mind the desire and the need of our less fortunate neighbours not to be left out. It would be shameful as well as potentially disastrous if we turned our cosy common market, social charter and all, into a protected space which raises borders where they must be lowered. Europe 1992 was, and is, important, but in economic terms at least it is only a part of the European Economic Space which includes the six remaining EFTA countries, and the beginning of a process which progressively encompasses the whole of Europe from the Atlantic coast to the Soviet borders.

It is less easy to see how such lofty ideals can be accomplished. Emergency assistance is fine and necessary, but it is no more than its name says. A Know-How Fund is useful, but it takes many years for know-how to be developed and applied. A Bank for European Recovery and Development may well help provide necessary capital, but even in the most favourable case, its effect will be as mixed, and as slow as that of the Marshall Plan. Private business has a major role to play as soon as the legal conditions for its functioning have been created. But the deeper one goes into such questions of economic co-operation, the clearer it is that unless and until there are stable and convertible currencies, progress is bound to remain limited. This raises a key question – the key question of this article: how does one create a European Monetary Space? Is it the end of a long road, or can it stand at its beginning, or somewhere in the middle?

The German events which are taking place before our very eyes (and which still move at a pace which makes one apprehensive about mentioning them because they seem to run away from every author) are of great significance in this respect. They are also confusing, and probably unique.

In the mid 1950s, the now much quoted Article 23 of the West German Basic Law which enables 'parts of Germany' to accede to the Federal Republic, was invoked for the first time to enable the Saarland to join. After the war, the Saar Territory had been separated from the French zone of occupation and turned into a politically 'independent', economically French 'country'. It is debatable whether this 'country' (which joined not just the Council of Europe but also the European Coal and Steel Community as a full member) was ever viable, though it seemed quite viable to me when I arrived in 1954 to live there and teach at the *Université de la Sarre* with its French Rector and its international staff. However, none of this was to last very long.

The turbulent year 1954 saw among other significant changes – such as the failure of the European Defence Community and Germany's membership of NATO – an agreement between Mendes-France and Adenauer to hold a referendum in the Saar in 1955. The result was nearly a foregone conclusion; I fought on the losing side at the time and supported Europeanisation of the Saar, but the people wanted accession to the Federal Republic. France accepted the verdict; a transition was negotiated. This transition involved political union with the Federal Republic on 1 January 1957, but continued economic union with France projected to last for another three years and later shortened to two-and-a-half. In other words, from the beginning of 1957 to the middle of 1959 a German Land operated with French currency and a curiously intermediate fiscal and customs system. For the people of the Saar, this was not a bad condition to be in. In Eastern Europe today, there are those whom the American financier-philanthropist George Soros likes to describe as 'arbitrageurs between systems', who may well be the only ones who benefit from the present uncertainties. In a sense, all Saarlanders were such arbitrageurs. Indeed, when full monetary union with West Germany was finally established in July 1959, many people in the Saar felt cheated despite the favourable exchange rate guaranteed by the Federal Government. It is said today that monetary union with the Saar cost West Germany 1.8 billion deutschmarks of the time, most of which went to France in one way or another; though I am never sure that such calculations tell an awful lot about real cost and real benefits.

The Saarland has one million inhabitants. Their standard of living in 1957 was not very dissimilar from that of other West Germans. They were also living in a fundamentally similar political, economic and legal system. After all, their independence had lasted less than a decade. Moreover, West Germany itself was only beginning to move into the top gear of economic development which was to make it the wealthiest country of Europe. Indeed, the convertibility of the Deutschmark was not yet fully established. East Germany today has some 16 million inhabitants. Their per capita income is unknown; all figures in international handbooks now turn out to be misleading exaggerations, it is probably more like one-fifth of that of West Germans than the one-half usually quoted. The East German economy is in a state of shambles. Many factories and other production facilities will have to be closed as soon as European standards of health, safety, let alone environment-friendliness are applied. Skilled workers are leaving the country in droves (and, which is not irrelevant, their skills are by no means immediately usable in the West; many require as much as a year's re-training). Most legal and practical preconditions of economic adjustment are lacking. In the absence of goods in the shops there is a significant monetary overhang. Great promises of social security have been made while services were antiquated and unsatisfactory. One could go on telling tales of misery. And yet there is now a German monetary union before any of these issues have been resolved, indeed before there is political union. Once East Germany as a whole, or its constituent *Lander*, invoke Article 23, many of the transitional developments which it took two-and-a-half years to work out in the case of the Saar may already have happened.

The reasons are familiar, yet important. They have to do with an unbearable socio-economic differential within one relevant political space. Since the breaching of the wall, Germans have for all practical purposes regarded the entire territory of the West and the East German republics as 'their' space. For West Germans, this means that while they enjoy their nostalgic trips to Goethe's Weimar, Luther's Eisenach and the resorts of the Baltic Sea, they also have to put up with a stream of East Germans who increasingly threaten their jobs and (oddly even more important though quite unreal) their homes. The over-riding West German question is: how can we be united and yet make sure that the 'brothers and sisters' stay at home? For East Germans, the common space means that they no longer compare their position with that of West Germans merely in abstract, but in specific and real terms.

Why should they earn so much less for the same work than the 'brothers and sisters' in the West? Such questions make for irresistible political pressure. One day, the story will be told of how the President of the *Bundesbank*, Karl Otto Pohl, had to eat his words and give in to a government which realised that a single German currency is the only hope of allaying social fears while satisfying national aspirations. When the story is told, we will also know a little more about the limits of the autonomy of a constitutionally independent central bank.

GEMU (as the *Economist* has styled German Economic and Monetary Union) has now happened. It is a messy and extra-ordinarily expensive process. Fortunately, West Germany can afford it.

Indeed, while the buyers of West German government bonds may moan, many others will watch with delight as the balance of payments surplus melts away and Germany is generally forced to apply its public and private wealth to others rather than its own protection. This may be, as some say, *reculer pour mieux sauter*, but the Federal Republic has to lean rather far back for a jump which could be thwarted by many unforeseen developments. Without doubt, the cost of GEMU is going to be much higher than 16 times the 1.8 billion marks which the integration of the Saarland cost thirty years ago. The monetary overhang of East Germany alone is about 50 billion marks, and savers have been given promises which make an exchange rate of one to one for a large part of personal savings almost an entitlement. Equally importantly, monetary union will add further momentum to political union, East Germans had to hand in their mint to the *Bundesbank* in Frankfurt. With the mint went economic policy more generally. Indeed, people elsewhere in Europe may well conclude from the German experience that you cannot have monetary union without political union.

I am not unaware of the fact that as I go on I am throwing more and more spanners into the works of EMU. At any rate, the process of economic and monetary union looks more and more complicated. In fact it is very complicated. Even without the German experiences of 1957 and 1990, we could have known this, for the European Community itself has been at the point before at which it finds itself today, and before I try to draw two or three conclusions from these forays into the realms of money and politics in Europe, I want to remind you of at least two aspects of the experience of the early 1970s.

In the spring of 1970 – almost three years before British entry – the Community declared the Common Market complete. The *Achèvement* of a single market was, to be sure, primarily about one of the four freedoms of 1992, the free movement of goods (and even as such incomplete); it was nevertheless a proud moment for Europe which enabled the Community to move on to its *approfondissement* by economic and monetary union, no less. Raymond Barre, who was then the Commissioner responsible for economics and finance, and a Council committee headed by the Luxembourg Prime Minister Pierre Werner, produced a *plan par étapes* which foresaw the creation of full monetary union in three stages, and within ten years. As I think back to that time (I was then the Commissioner responsible for foreign relations and foreign trade) two experiences stick in my mind which may well contain lessons for today.

The first experience is that of endless discussions in the Council of ministers of finance about the relationship between monetary and economic union. The protagonists were, of course, the ministers representing France and Germany, Valéry Giscard d'Estaing on one side, Karl Schiller and Helmut Schmidt on the other. Today, Giscard and Schmidt in particular would like to rewrite history and claim that they were always proponents of monetary union. In fact, as heads of government, they were to have much to do with setting up of the European Monetary System. But in the early 1970s, they stood at opposing ends, and were both sceptics. Giscard proposed the

Cartesian route: monetary union first, and everything else will follow, but national sovereignty has to be safeguarded. Schiller and Schmidt insisted on the harmonisation of economic policy first, and also on the need for an autonomous central bank. The compromises which they reached were precarious and unsatisfactory; above all, they did not extend much beyond Stage One, which, like today, is one of benevolent co-operation rather than union.

Since then, much has changed in Germany, but above all in France. The most important single change is that there is now a clear all-party consensus in France that inflation has to be fought with all available means, and that the battle is won only once it is down to zero. A new attitude to the relationship between government and central bank follows from this change; no longer is the Bank of France regarded as a mere department of the Ministry of Finance. Undoubtedly, other developments are relevant, not least the realisation that France and Germany are by far the most important trading partners for each other. As a result, the 'E' in EMU is no longer problematic for the opponents of 1970. The same is true for most other members of the European Community though not for Britain. Leaving the metaphysics of national sovereignty on one side, it was certainly true for a long time, and may still be true today that in Britain most leading politicians, and consequently all governments, quite like a little inflation. Alistair Home quotes Harold Macmillan as saying that 'encouraged by my old friend, Roy Harrod, I still resisted the idea of deflation as a permanent or even prolonged policy' in 1960. 'Deflation' is what others would call stability. But such stability would, in the British view, discourage entrepreneurs and reduce the flexibility of governments. Macmillan again: 'So Keynes always said, between 2.5% to 3%, then nobody would notice... And this we achieved.' Could it be that by today the figures of acceptable inflation have slipped a little, to between 4% and 5%? However that may be, there are certain policy assumptions in Britain which are directly related to the role of the Treasury and the Bank, and which affect the ability of the country to join in European monetary co-operation. Put differently, and using Brandon Rhys Williams's phrase, even joining the EMS makes little sense 'while we continue to run our affairs more or less as before'.

My second memory of Europe's first plan to create monetary union in stages is more dramatic. After a year of planning and preparation, the Council of Ministers decided on 9 February 1971 that monetary union would be achieved by 1980. Stage One would start as soon as possible. On 27 April 1971, the ministers of finance of the then six member states decided to reduce the permissible margins of fluctuation between their currencies (from 1.5 to 1.2 per cent). Twelve days later, on 9 May 1971, the central banks of Germany and the Netherlands decided to allow their currencies to float. On 15 August 1971, the international monetary system of the post-war era collapsed when President Nixon and his Treasury Secretary, Connally, announced the suspension of the convertibility of the dollar into gold. After months of negotiation, the Smithsonian Agreement of 18 December 1971 aspired to provide some new stability, a 'tunnel' of discipline for currency fluctuations. For a while, the countries of the European Community tried to enforce an even stricter discipline; this was the time in which the European 'snake' wiggled about in the world 'tunnel'. But by 1973 it was clear that none of these mechanisms would work, and that the first project of European monetary union had died a quiet death.

What is the point of this unhappy reminder? It is above all one of insight. There is a qualitative difference between a customs union and a monetary union. Even the ambitious objectives of a single market in the emphatic sense of Europe 1992 can be achieved by decisions taken within a certain, circumscribed economic and political space. The four freedoms are by and large subjects of autonomous political decisions by the European Community and its members. In earlier days, when tariffs were the most important trade barrier, it made sense to speak of the creation of a customs union in stages, and of a final point at which all internal tariffs would be dismantled. None of this applies to monetary union. Money, convertible money at any rate, is enmeshed in complex and worldwide networks of relations which cannot be controlled by governments or by central banks either unilaterally or co-operatively. Even the European Community cannot hope to impose its own calendar on the progress of monetary co-operation. Things can happen which upset the best-designed plan for monetary union, and, as Murphy's Law tells us, whatever can happen to upset things, will happen.

Other points could be made in relation to the experience of the early 1970s. Money has much to do with power. What we call a monetary system, is much more likely to be a hegemonial system. The Bretton Woods system was backed by the US dollar, which is why 15 August 1971 marked such an important turning point. At that time, a process of disintegration began which, according to some, has now led to the emergence of three centres of power, built around the dollar, the yen, and the – yes, the what? The ecu? It is a mere basket of currencies. The German mark? Perhaps, but no one quite wants to admit it.

Thus we are back to European monetary union, European political integration, and a few conclusions from past and present experiences. The *first* conclusion is that in the absence of a functioning world order, it is important to create a zone of stability in Europe. This is true not just for money and trade, but in general political terms. It is also meant precisely as it is put here. I for one have never regarded European union as a purpose in itself. I am not dreaming of a European superstate.

Ultimately, only worldwide rules can guarantee liberty and peace, justice and prosperity. But at the moment we cannot have such rules. We therefore need an optimum of European co-operation in areas of policy in which sovereignty has long left national shores and borders. Europe 1992 is a step in the right direction, especially if it remains open for the wider European Economic Space and for post-communist Europe. The 1992 project will have to be followed by a new *approfondissement*, and the two most important subjects for intensified European co-operation are defence, and money.

The second conclusion is that monetary union defies planning of the 1992 variety. It is important to be clear about the objective, and about the next step; but any detailed timetable of progress is likely to be put off by unexpected events and then lead to disappointments and doubts. German monetary union is, in fact, one such unexpected event. It is understandable that the other members of the EMS and the Delors Commission insist on the Community staying on course for further monetary co-operation, and the inter-governmental conference to define the next steps will still probably be set up later this year. Moreover, the Federal Republic in both its present and its likely future shape will clearly wish to demonstrate its European commitment by going along with proposals for progress. But given the important role of the German mark – and of the Federal Bank – in this process, and the extent to which both are likely to be strained by GEMU, it is physically impossible to advance as quickly as President Mitterrand and his ministers would like to move. Even expert time will be in short supply, let alone the funds required for a transition which, like all change, is bound to have an initial cost.

There are other problems. It is said that the Swiss Central Bank is upset not only about being left out of the co-ordination meetings of Central Bank governors, which take place on Swiss territory at the Bank for International Settlements in Basle, but above all about no longer being kept informed even by traditional friends when important decisions are taken. This may be so, but the Swiss franc remains one of the currencies for which Brandon Rhys Williams's description is appropriate that they are neither large enough to compete with dollar and yen nor small enough to be purely subordinate. The same is true for the Austrian schilling and the Swedish crown, both of which have to be reckoned with in any plan for monetary integration. And then, of course, there is the pound sterling which cannot be ignored even if Britain remains somewhat detached from European developments.

This is not an argument against the Delors Plan, but it is an interpretation of its real significance. The objective of full monetary union in Europe makes sense as one looks into the future of international economic relations. But this objective is not likely to be achieved for some time to come. *In* the meantime, the Saar route is more relevant than the GDR route. This, of course, is shorthand and, therefore, misleading. What I mean is that in the case of Europe, there is no compelling reason or interest for rushing into monetary union as the two Germanies are doing under our eyes. There is, however, every reason for taking the steps which at the end of the day make the introduction of a common currency an almost technical issue. These steps include ever closer monetary co-operation as well as co-ordinated economic, fiscal, budgetary policies and some of the 'flanking policies' aiming at greater social and regional balance, which are quite justly the subject of much debate. It is nice, and probably right, to think in systematic terms about such an array of common policies for Europe; but their implementation will not be systematic. Stage Two (if it has to be) should be about being prepared for the moment at which it is both possible and desirable to create full monetary union. This stage will, therefore, be much less systematic than some Cartesian planners want it to be, but much more substantial than those who are worried about the whole process are prepared to accept at the moment.

The *third* conclusion has to do with the title of this article, and notably with the relation between money and politics. It is my most hesitant conclusion. The Saarland had realised political union with the Federal Republic before there was monetary union; Luxembourg has long had a monetary union with Belgium without political union. Hong Kong is hoping for a Saar solution with a 50-year transition period. Countries like Singapore have pegged their currency to the dollar while staying as independent politically as Luxembourg. A European Monetary Union with a common currency and one Central Bank is conceivable which does not alter the role of the Queen, or even the Queen in Parliament very much, though perhaps Jean Monnet's head will appear on the ecu notes – or the *monnets*, as some have suggested – issued by the autonomous European central bank.

This is not to minimise the problem. EMU is a very serious proposition. If European Defence Union of some sorts were to be added, the national political space would lose much, though by no means all, of its relevance. But it is losing relevance in any ease. Sovereignty is not a commodity which one can keep or relinquish at will. The greatest productive force of our time, the transnational enterprise, has long escaped the grip of governmental institutions, whether national or European. Who now controls the flow of capital in the world? Who can even allocate trade to national statistics? Nor is this merely true for money and trade. What exactly is 'national defence' in the nuclear age? And whose sovereign decision making body controls the great issues of the environment, or of development? In a sense, therefore, it is undoubtedly true that the Europeanisation of monetary sovereignty is a part of a wider process which will detract from traditional political spaces.

7

Europe Must Avoid the American Model

Janet Daley, 1989.

*Janet Daley was a regular correspondent for **The Times** who now writes for **The Daily Telegraph**. She is the author of **Honourable Friends**.*

THE argument for European federation in its most extreme form seems to be advocating a union of sovereign states, the tacit model for which is the United States of America. The case being put forward is suspect on two different levels. On the one hand, it seems to assume that the American system is itself unproblematic while at the same time proposing a degree of unification more extreme even than that of the American states. The package being offered seems oddly incoherent and naive.

It is quite wrongheaded to conceive of the North American aggregation of original colonies and territorial acquisitions, partially administered by a central government whose powers have grown in a higgledy-piggledy fashion never envisaged by the founding fathers, as an exemplar of perfectly delegated sovereignty. In the historical experience of the US, a confederation of independently governed states is, in fact, riddled with contradictions. It succeeds (or at least, does not disintegrate) only to the extent that every new political generation finds an equilibrium between federal intervention and state sovereignty which outrages the fewest pressure groups. Ever since Abraham Lincoln waged civil war against the southern states to stop them seceding from the Union, there has been more or less explicit conflict between the interests and sympathies of state and federal authorities. Until recent presidencies like those of Carter and Reagan, antipathy to Washington's power remained deeply ingrained in the South where the federal government was regarded as essentially a northern outfit attempting to foist urban liberal values on the stately old agrarian Confederacy.

In the sixties, civil rights disputes (most notably over school desegregation) made the shibboleth of 'states' rights' an unsavoury cover for racist policies, but the tension between centralized control and state autonomy is a permanent fixture of American political life. Its endless debates and temporary resolutions provide a lesson for Europeans who see constitutional unification as an idyll of rationality and consensus.

In terms of the current European debate, it is of particular interest that those areas of public life which have proved almost irreconcilable to national agreement have been issues of social policy: not only racial discrimination but the treatment of criminality (i.e. capital punishment) and personal morality (abortion). The attempts to produce a consistent national position on questions like these have come closer to tearing the country apart than has any external threat. To see why the superimposition of a national policy on, say, capital punishment, is so explosively contentious, it is necessary to understand that every state in the US is in charge of its own criminal law. The policing, judiciary and criminal justice systems of each state are independent of one another to the extent that a criminal (unless wanted for a specifically *federal* offence) can escape prosecution simply by crossing the state boundary – a fact immortalised in many a Hollywood film.

When the murders of civil rights workers threatened to go unpunished in the southern state where they were committed, the recourse for an outraged federal government was a roundabout appeal to the Constitution. By defining the killing of a person as the ultimate deprivation of his civil rights, murder could be classified as a federal offence and thereby come under Washington's jurisdiction. This kind of circuitous legalism constantly bedevils a federation of sovereign states affiliated by a written constitution. The US has not only to cope with the conflicting views of its member states but with the encumbrance of a two centuries-old constitution whose authority exceeds that of any elected government. What the Lockean idealists who wrote it failed to anticipate (legislation to prevent racial discrimination, for example) has since had to be laboriously and protractedly appended to their antique structure. Such a permanently installed document, essential in a federation of quasi-independent states, becomes a cumbersome, reactionary monolith which slows government response to public opinion, sometimes fatally.

Among the cruellest examples of this must be the fate of the Equal Rights Amendment to the Constitution. Formulated in the heat of the women's movement of the seventies, it sought to provide protection against sexual discrimination. But any such amendment to the Constitution must be ratified by a two-thirds majority of the states of the Union. The Equal Rights Amendment crawled through exhausting and expensive campaigns in one state after another, finally dying from lack of the necessary majority when its deadline was reached for ratification. By contrast, Britain, responding to the overwhelming social pressure of the period, adopted a Sex Discrimination Act almost identical in force to the Equal Rights Amendment, within the lifetime of a single parliament. It is ironic that the US, the birthplace of contemporary feminism, should have no national sex discrimination legislation. It is a cautionary tale for those advocating the social unification of Europe whose own bloodcurdling history of religious and moral disputes makes the social contradictions of the American states look benign. Are there contemporary politicians so credulous as to believe that appeals to an enshrined constitution and supra-national Bill of Rights could settle differences of profoundly rooted national outlook? Or that ancient disputes over moral values will not be reinvigorated by forceable uniformity? In the United States, there is an absolute separation of church and state which makes the strictly secular nature of political life incontrovertible. Could Catholic countries which prohibit the sale of contraceptives (or legal divorce) ever be persuaded to adopt such a clear-cut division between the jurisdiction of the Church and the law? And if they did not, how parallel with the American model could European federation hope to be?

The very notion of democracy varies among European states, unlike the United States of America which was inaugurated by a coherent and concerted act. Born out of enlightenment political theory, the US was created on the premise that an ideal state could be constructed from scratch out of rational mechanisms. The idea may seem quaint from our vantage point (although it presumably does not to all those trusting pro-European fantasists) but at least in forming a union out of fledgling colonies the Americans were starting with a clean slate. Imposing a pan-European political unity on the established detritus of hundreds (or thousands) of years of enmity, cultural differentiation and religious opposition speaks more of madness than innocence. France's republicanism, with its legalistic formality and self-conscious theorising is quite unlike Britain's parliamentary tradition. The British concept of democracy predates the French revolution. Emerging from Magna Carta it has evolved through centuries of organic growth to produce an extraordinarily adaptable and responsive form of government. How long would it be before these distinct inherited conceptions themselves were seen as obstacles to ultimate cohesiveness?

Where the American union seems least troubled is in its delegation of taxation responsibilities. Here there is a telling contrast with the Eurofederalist lobby. Americans pay a universal federal income tax to support the programmes of national government. They also pay state taxes which vary enormously depending on the political complexion of the state government and its internal spending needs for infrastructure and social services. Each state organises its economy on its own fiscal and social priorities. Nevada receives enough revenue from its legalised gambling industry to make personal state taxes virtually non-existent, whereas New York, with its enormous inner city problems, levies high state taxes. Decisions about what form and level this taxation should take are made internally and idiosyncratically, producing occasional anomalies. (Crossing the state line to buy cheaper liquor is an old American custom.) Indirect taxes, notably sales taxes, are imposed by many states, but are not universal. That is to say, the completely free market in goods and services which prevails between states in the US is quite unhampered by the absence of standardised point-of-sale taxation (which we call VAT).

It is quite true that this lack of uniformity creates inequalities for producers of the kind feared by Jacques Delors. It is more expensive to produce and sell goods in some parts of the country than in others. What this means is that, in practice, the market must sort itself out. Industry has had to move from the more costly areas to the cheaper and more spacious (which often meant further west) and labour has had to move with it. Most significantly, poorer areas which marketed cheaper goods had a chance to increase their regional wealth by their extra competitiveness. The American experience suggests that the operation of a deregulated free market between independent states is thoroughly feasible without harmonisation of indirect taxes. What is much more dubious is the social and political merger of distinct regions with their own social histories. If the US, with its common language and degree of cultural homogeneity, finds this problem so daunting, what can be the prospect for Europe with its tenaciously individual national identities?

8

1988 –
Britain's Year of the Dutch

Christie Davies, 1989.

Christie Davies is Professor of Sociology at the University of Reading.

BY chance we are, in 1988, celebrating the anniversaries of two occasions in our history when serious threats to our national independence and Parliamentary democracy were averted thanks largely to the help of the Dutch. I refer of course to the defeat of the Spanish Armada sent to invade and conquer England and Wales in 1588 and to the Glorious Revolution of 1688 which not only secured the foundations of democracy in Britain, but later was to inspire the American Revolution, Constitution and Bill of Rights. Had it not been for the courage and decision of the Dutch in 1588 and 1688, today Britain would not be a democracy and might even not exist.

Our traditional British myth about the Armada is that we, Europe's off-shore islanders, stood alone against Imperial Spain much as we later did against Napoleon and Hitler. We have long believed that the Armada was defeated by our nimbler and more skilful British warships under the command of men like Sir Francis Drake. The tale of Drake calmly continuing his game of bowls on Plymouth Hoe, after being told that the Spanish Armada had been sighted in the English Channel is one that every child used to be taught at school as an example of British coolness and understatement in the face of over-whelming odds. Drake's activities as a pirate who attacked the Spanish treasure fleet and looted Latin American cities though are glossed over with ambiguous terms such as 'privateer'. Today, as befits good Europeans, we have come to acknowledge that we owe much of the victory that saved us from invasion to our allies the Dutch 'sea-beggars' whose little ships blockaded the mouth of the Scheldt and the coast of Flanders.

The Armada that came from Spain was not itself the invasion force but a powerful naval escort for the Duke of Parma's army which was to travel in barges from Dunkirk across the narrow seas to England. It was the same army that had been fighting for many years against the determination of the Dutch to declare themselves independent from the rule of the Spanish Hapsburgs. Indeed, it was our support for this early war of national liberation that provoked Philip II of Spain to invade England in the hope that his daughter would supplant Elizabeth as Queen. Thus, the independence of our two small countries on the far north-western periphery of Europe was achieved by our mutual aid for one another. If we had failed in 1588, instead of a modern European Community of freely co-operating equals, there would be only the colonial deadness of spirit that still afflicts Latin-America. Furthermore, the United States and Canada would be under the autocratic rule of the imperial viceroy in Mexico City.

Exactly a hundred years later the Dutch again saved Britain. When Charles II died without a legitimate son, his brother James II who succeeded him proved to be an autocrat with no respect for Britain's unwritten constitutional principles and conventions. A group of British notables now approached William of Orange, the ruler of the Netherlands and husband of James' daughter Mary, and he invaded England with a

Dutch army. James fled and William and Mary became joint sovereigns in what is still called the 'Glorious Revolution'. William's new Parliament now permanently established the basic democratic principle of 'no taxation without representation'. It was a *Dutch* king of England who accepted this principle that in the past had caused the English Civil War and which was later to spark off the Boston tea-party and the American Revolution. From now on only Parliament and not the King had the power to tax the people, a fact which saved us from the cycle of absolutism and revolution that was to engulf France. William's Parliament also passed a Bill of Rights which was later to become the basis for one of the most crucial amendments to the American Constitution.

The relations between Britain and the Netherlands have not always been smooth as can be seen from the terms that have entered the English language as a result of past trade rivalry and naval clashes. Even today anything incomprehensible is called double Dutch. Dutch silver is a cheap alloy. Dutch courage is acquired by getting drunk, a Dutch uncle is far from avuncular and the guests at a Dutch treat are forced to 'go Dutch'. In 1988 though, it is the Dutch ally that has so often saved the British people from defeat and tyranny, that is being celebrated, the same Dutch who fought with Marlborough against Louis XIV and with Wellington at Waterloo, the Dutch whose gallant fight against the Nazi invader in 1940 helped to enable the British army to escape from Dunkirk.

For the British people, the Dutch have not only proved their worth as warriors, but as peacemakers. Almost alone of the nations of Europe they have tried to seek a constructive solution to the conflict between the Protestants and Catholics in Northern Ireland. Where others have only criticised, the Dutch have tried to provide reconciliation. The Netherlands itself has in the past had to solve the problem of integrating the Roman Catholic half of its population into an originally and officially Calvinist state. This was achieved without bloodshed through the creation of a uniquely Dutch 'pillarised' society where each religious or secular-political community has its own autonomous institutions. If William of Orange's kinsmen can find a way for the Ulster Orangemen, who still march under the banner of 'King Billy' to live in harmony with their Roman Catholic neighbours, we will once again owe an enormous debt to our helpful Dutch neighbour. In Britain in 1988 care is being taken not to celebrate past victories in a way that might give offence to or create hostility against the Spanish, French or Irish, all former antagonists who are now our partners in the European Community. The unity and harmony of Europe demands that ancient clashes and enmities should be forgotten rather than celebrated with old fashioned triumphalism. However, there is no need to consign the alliances and friendships of the past to oblivion in this way and that is why we should treat 1988 as the year of the Dutch.

9

The Future of Europe

Ted Dunn, 1989.

Ted Dunn is the author of **Step by Step to World Peace** *and author or editor of numerous other works.*

THE speed with which events are taking place in Eastern Europe may be compared with 1947 when Europe faced the prospect of economic disaster and new institutions were created almost overnight. Then, the US stepped in and gave Europe over 2% of its GNP in grant form for four years with the result that for the first time in history all the countries in Western Europe co-operated and laid the foundations for a prosperous and peaceful region.

Today, although everyone admires the concept of glasnost the unfortunate fact is that the economic base upon which it depends is threatening to disintegrate and remove Mr. Gorbachov and all he stands for. Similar problems affect most of the other Eastern European countries. If this trend continues and disaffection becomes explosive the whole of Eastern Europe may be thrown into turmoil destroying our recently raised hopes for a peaceful Europe. Clearly it is in our own interests to do all we can, while there is still time, to support Mr. Gorbachov.

Two requirements are needed for success. First, that we have a clear understanding about the kind of structure we want for Europe, and second, the means to enable this vision to become a reality.

The structure of Europe

What everyone is afraid of is a Europe divided into two powerful antagonistic halves each fearful of the other, with tariffs keeping us apart and an arms race continuing into the future with all the risks that implies. Nor do we want a Europe where too much power is placed at the centre because history has shown that power corrupts and absolute power corrupts absolutely. Giving more power to the EEC for instance, may seem a good idea today under reasonable leaders, but that power could easily become excessively authoritarian and be misused in the future.

The alternative is to decentralize power as much as possible while at the same time encouraging co-operation at every level with power residing at the bottom: in other words our task is to achieve unity with diversity. This is a vision that could be achieved by encouraging the two halves of Germany to retain their own separate identities and the divided Berlin to become united as a Free City. These three constituents of Germany could co-operate through their respective regional organisations, and with each other, under the auspices of the Council of Europe. This principle of unity with diversity could be extended to other countries of Europe seeking their independence, i.e. Scotland and the Basque country: the example of Switzerland and its Cantons is to be commended.

Few people seem to recognise the importance of the Council of Europe yet it could be the ideal organisation for enabling Gorbachov's vision of a 'European family' to be realised, without creating a power bloc, or threatening anyone. It was an idea that Churchill conceived during the war and brought to fruition in 1949 following the commencement of the Marshall Plan in 1947 with the aims of:

'working for greater European unity; for the principles of parliamentary democracy; for the rule of law and human rights; to improve living conditions and promote human values.'

The Council's Statute also declares that each member state must recognise the principle of the rule of law and guarantee its citizens the enjoyment of human rights and fundamental freedoms. The scope of the Council covers practically all aspects of European affairs except defence, based on the ideals of the UN Declaration of Human Rights.

The most notable of its achievements has been to establish the European Court of Human Rights to which the 22 member states have voluntarily sacrificed a remarkable degree of their sovereignty in the rule of law; one of the greatest achievements of modern times. Membership of the Council of Europe is already nearly double the number of countries in the EEC and includes the Nordic and EFTA countries. Poland and Hungary may soon join provided they agree to the principles outlined above.

Despite the fact that the Council of Europe has only moral power to enforce its decisions, the fact remains that most, if not all, decisions reached by the European Court of Human Rights have been observed and implemented, especially by Britain, the worst offender, because of the number of times she has been taken to the Court. Unfortunately there is now talk of Britain derogating from the European Human Rights Convention just at a time when it is most urgently needful of our support.

Many important European Conventions have been signed, the most important being the Convention on Human Rights and the European Social Charter. More recently (June 26, 1987) the European Convention for the Prevention of Torture (inhuman or degrading treatment or punishment) came into force and established a committee to visit any place without necessarily having first received a complaint about torture. These Conventions are now widely regarded as the yardstick by which to judge the conduct of its members; they demand our whole-hearted support.

Despite the success of the Council of Europe, it is the EEC that gains all the attention of governments. So much so that it is threatening to separate us economically, and possibly politically, from true co-operation with other countries outside Western Europe. A 'Fortress Europe' is a real possibility. The individual is also threatened with a loss of meaning, purpose and identity, all in the cause of 'harmonisation'.

Economic co-operation between members of the EEC is of course important, but the rule of law to safeguard our freedoms and human rights within the Council of Europe is far more important. Within this concept a new vision of co-operation with Eastern Europe becomes possible. Eastern European countries should therefore be encouraged to join the Council of Europe as soon as possible. Mr. Gorbachov already talks about becoming a part of the 'European family' and this vision could be realised within the concept of the Council of Europe. An Eastern European regional development programme, based on Marshall Plan principles, would nurture Eastern European social, economic and political institutions within a European concept to which both East and West owe their allegiance. More importantly, co-operation based on a spirit of generosity would increase trust and confidence and dispel the fears that have bedevilled us for so long.

The advantage of seeking the future of all Europe within the Council of Europe is that it would deter countries from 'playing politics' with each other. Instead of competing we would be co-operating for the good of all within a framework of organisation that observes the rule of law based on social, economic and political justice. It would be a voluntary association of countries bound together for their individual mutual benefit.

To avoid too much centralisation of power, countries with common regional interests (e.g. those bordering the Mediterranean or the North Sea) could make separate treaties specifically applicable to their own region. Eastern Europe could retain its Council for Mutual Economic Assistance (CMEA) and Western Europe its EEC but more localised agreements should be encouraged; for instance, Berlin could become a Free City with its own government, as proposed by Mr. Khruschev as a solution to the Berlin crisis before the Wall was built. This idea was unfortunately dismissed by the West and led, some believe, directly to Khruschev's removal from office.

To avoid unnecessary conflict over the future of military alliances between NATO and the Warsaw Pact countries, they should be allowed to wither away, or become purely defensive concepts. If co-operation is emphasised, along the lines advocated in this article, their importance would diminish, buttressed by Conventions agreed within the Council of Europe.

An Eastern European Marshall Plan

The vision of a 'European family' under the rule of law, however, cannot be achieved unless there is economic, social and political stability in Eastern Europe. This was the prerequisite condition for peaceful relationships in Western Europe in 1947 that led naturally to the Council of Europe and the formation of the EEC; but it was only made possible by the Marshall Plan. As Dean Acheson, one of its main architects said:

> 'Until the various countries of the world get on their feet and become self-supporting there can be no political or economic stability in the world and no lasting peace for any of us.'

This is as true today as in 1947. The moral is obvious: we should initiate something similar now.

The recent Paris meeting of prime ministers has taken the first encouraging step in this direction by pledging funds for

Eastern Europe. If these funds are insufficient, however, or given (as seems likely) in loan form, or to individual countries outside any comprehensive regional concept, it is probable that the help given will fail and may even do more harm than good.

Before aid is given it is very important to appreciate the principles upon which the Marshall Plan was built and I can do no better than quote from George Marshall's historic address in 1947:

> 'Our policy is not against any country or doctrine but against hunger, poverty, desperation and chaos. Its purpose should be the revival of a working economy in the world so as to permit the emergence of political and social conditions in which free institutions can exist. Such assistance, I am convinced, must not be on a piecemeal basis as various crises develop. Any assistance that this government may render in the future should provide a cure rather than a mere palliative...

> 'It would be neither fitting nor efficacious for this government to undertake to draw up unilaterally a program designed to place Europe on its feet economically. That is the business of the Europeans. The initiative must come from Europe. The role of this country should consist of friendly aid in the drafting of a European program and of later support of such program as far as is practical for us to do so. The program should be a joint one, agreed to by a number, if not all of the European nations.'

From this speech it will be clear that aid was given to the region, not to any one country. The region itself was asked to formulate the development programme. Its implementation was helped by a Secretariat composed of individuals who were not politicians, but individuals in whom all the countries concerned had confidence. The aim of the Plan was to 'provide a cure rather than a mere palliative'. The Marshall Plan was offered to all Europe, including Russia, but it fell foul of the Cold War, some sceptics say, to the relief of the US. Nevertheless it was a brilliant success.

Today, 42 years later, we have the opportunity of recapturing the vision of a truly united and peaceful Europe. During these years the UN has established itself as the ideal organisation to implement a second Marshall Plan. The UN Development Programme could undertake the task but it would be even better to initiate a new agency, which might be called the UN Peace and Development Fund. Europe offers the key to world peace based on co-operation with the USSR. This would release vast resources to initiate similar regional peace and development programmes in other regions of the world in desperate need.

Working through the UN has many advantages, not least because it would encourage all nations, particularly Japan, the US (as in 1947) and the oil countries to participate. If these countries fail to support the idea, however, Western Europe should follow the example of the US by unilaterally financing the development programme itself. It is important to work through the UN because it provides a neutral base and avoids the possibility of the development programme being misunderstood. Work through UN agencies such as GATT (General Agreement on Tariffs and Trade) and support of the idea of an International Criminal Court to uphold the Nuremburg Principles should also be encouraged. So far as possible we should work locally but within a regional and world perspective recognising that 'no man is an island'. Ultimately it is only through the UN that world peace will be established and therefore it is important to work through structures that encourage this objective.

Finding funds should present no real problem if we consider that the peace and future of Europe is at stake. These funds could be found by responding to Mr. Gorbachov's pleas for faster disarmament – a process that could release money at present being spent by both Eastern and Western Europe on armaments. Several years ago the USSR made a proposal, in the UN, for 10% of all money saved from disarmament to be used to support development. This proposal was supported in the General Assembly by 83 votes to only 2 against. I suggest that our government should implement this resolution immediately. Additional funds could be found by using the huge sums owed by many countries to finance their internal economic well-being. As these sums will probably never be repaid anyway it would be far better to make a virtue out of necessity and cancel the debt in exchange for support for a regional development programme.

The fact that Britain also urgently needs more money for many of its social services should not prevent us giving generous aid, because a peaceful Europe, based on a process of disarmament, means large sums of money being released to enable us to finance both the Eastern bloc and our own needs. This is a task far more urgent than the Falklands campaign which took billions of pounds out of our contingency reserves to the detriment of our economy. If several of the richer nations gave similar sums of money the peace of Europe, and possibly the world, could be assured, with all the benefits that would bring.

No matter how generous Western aid may be, however, the only real way of funding Eastern European countries' problems must be by the USSR making big savings from disarmament. We hold the key to Mr. Gorbachov's success by enabling him to achieve this objective. Failure to act now could bring disaster.

The imperative need is for us to have the vision and a generosity of spirit without which nothing can be accomplished. The Marshall Plan demonstrated that this vision is not an impossible dream but a practical realistic possibility. But if we do not act soon perestroika may fail and our opportunity will be lost.

10

Is Mrs Thatcher's Europe Realisable?

Douglas Evans, 1989.

Douglas Evans is an author, journalist and international economic consultant.

FOR so long has the Prime Minister forthrightly asserted the British interest in Europe that when in September she enunciated at Bruges the vision she has for the future of the Community it was widely interpreted on the Continent and at home as yet another assertion of British sovereignty. Commission President Jacques Delors made a strong riposte from Mrs. Thatcher inevitable when he asserted (and subsequently repeatedly reasserted) his belief that within ten years eighty per cent of the principal economic decisions would be taken in Brussels and that an 'embryo European government' was not far off.

No doubt it was yet another assertion of the British interest; no doubt it was the opening salvo in the campaign for this year's Euro-elections. But it was much more than this as an examination of her five listed objectives makes clear. These objectives – the willing and active cooperation among independent and sovereign states; a practical approach to Community problems, especially farm policy; the encouragement of enterprise by deregulation; a single market open to the world; a more active role by the Community members of NATO – are not only unexceptional but they offer a vision of Europe in tune with contemporary economic experience and Euro-strategic realities seen in the context of the global environment. In short Mrs. Thatcher's speech is a milestone because it represents not only her first statement of her overall European vision since Britain's signing of the Single European Act, and a clear assertion of the primary importance of preserving national sovereignty and the supremacy of parliamentary institutions over economic bodies, but a preliminary appeal to forge a pan-European alliance based on principles which could well extend outside the Community.

The point which seems to have been widely ignored in Mrs. Thatcher's speech is that without deserting her commitment to greater economic co-operation within the Community (where she clearly favours the creation of an effective and comprehensive free trade area, a concept which is currently emerging in North America and Australasia), she has espoused a vision of Europe that is as much cultural as political and economic. It is because EC officials have so long assiduously defined Europe within the confines of the Treaty of Rome that they choose to ignore this dimension. It was Britain's commitment to this wider Europe, claims Mrs. Thatcher, that led Britain to fight two costly European wars this century and to continue maintaining 70,000 troops on the Continent to avert another. If that third conflict is to be averted, the Prime Minister insists, Europe must be so constructed that it can retain its Atlantic ties and yet build bridges to the peoples of Eastern Europe. In a word, the Community within which Britain wishes to participate must be outward looking or it will never fulfill its political destiny.

Much of the Prime Minister's Bruges speech will strike a chord with the British people. In their assertion of parliamentary sovereignty Conservatives could, as the pre-eminent party of patriotism, increasingly draw off Labour supporters on this issue which could readily reveal many traditional Labour voters patriots first and socialists second, as in the Falklands War. More immediately, the Prime Minister faces a threefold challenge.

Firstly, her speech confronts the doctrine of the historical inevitability of the development of political and economic union with an implicit counter-doctrine, namely that the forces of economic globalization and of national cultural resurgence are far stronger than the procrustean framework that the Community's founding fathers first envisaged. The spectacular growth in technology, trade and financial flows notably stimulated the world economy far beyond the mental horizons of the European fathers while the very process of industrialism has created a need for human roots in a distinctive national identity. Moreover, it is perfectly understandable that after their painful experiences in the last war and the years prior to its outbreak the leaders of West Germany and Italy should embrace the idea of pooled sovereignty so willingly. The French, by contrast, like the British inheritors of an extended experience of nationhood, have been more open to the concept of economic and political union, on the unspoken understanding that it would adopt mostly French forms and traditions. To the extent that there was a single European tradition in modern times it was Napoleonic.

Secondly, it challenges both a minority of British ministers and a significant number of federalist or at least corporatist inclined British Euro-MPs as to the direction the Community should take. In practice it has long been arguable that the Community's institutions and concepts of unification are obsolete. More particularly they have been overtaken by the instrument of the multinational companies, among the primary generators of worldwide growth, but also by the economic and cultural globalization that has been a feature of the last thirty years, that is since the Community was formed. It has been observed many times, that rather as the socialism drawn up in Britain during the war years was out of date by 1945, so the concept and institutions of the Community's founding fathers were obsolete by 1957. Again and again these institutions have proved themselves incapable of changing course once their compass has been set whatever the circumstances, the monstrosities of the Common Agricultural Policy offering the prime example. Such characteristics are not uncommon features of societies slow to respond to democratic demands.

Thirdly, there is the challenge of allowing Germany to discover its permanent place both in Europe and the world. One of the reasons that Chancellor Kohl, as much as Jacques Delors, seems bent on advancing the integration of the Community as rapidly as possible is that West Germany remains politically less self-confident than her economic strength might suggest. The *Europe des Patries*, the Germans (excepting the late Franz Josef Strauss) argue, might suit the French and British with their long history of national independence and parliamentary supremacy, but suits West Germany and Italy much less well. Indeed, the joint statement of five Christian Democrats (i.e. Catholic) leaders of West Germany, Belgium, Luxembourg, the Netherlands, and Italy underlines what has long been ignored, the preponderance of predominantly Catholic nations with a continental as well as national cultural consciousness. Spain, Portugal and Ireland are even more explicitly Catholic countries but with less commitment to cultural continentalism.

Given that she seems so heavily outnumbered by the majority consensus currently prevailing among other European leaders in favour of rapid political as well as economic integration – something she was not unaware of when she first blew the trumpets at Bruges – what is the Prime Minister trying to achieve?

Firstly, and most transparently, she seems distinctly disinclined to disregard (as are some who make great play of their sense of destiny) Britain's one thousand years of unbroken independent rule reinforced by three centuries of uninterrupted parliamentary supremacy and is bent on the preservation of both as far as she is able. An expanded free trade area with the closest possible collaboration among European nations is clearly more to her taste than a centralised European superstate.

Secondly, she is fully aware that the economic liberalisation of Britain is far from complete and could swiftly be undermined by aspects of the centralised European state that are already visible over the horizon, ranging from a European central bank, a common currency, common standards for workers' rights and a strong possibility that many of the new common standards will create barriers to outside competition. The helter-skelter rush of US, Japanese and Australasian companies, not to mention their Far Eastern newly industrialised cousins, to gain a commercial foothold in the Community before 1992 only underscores their fears of external trade barriers.

This leads naturally to the Prime Minister's third objective, to focus the attention of the Community outward rather than inward in commercial as well as defence terms by warning against the 'Fortress Europe' mentality in the economic sphere and suggesting that this has a direct linkage with our vital interest in maintaining a powerful US military presence in Europe. Most recently the indecent haste in which West European banking consortia, replete with government guarantees, have been offering commercial credits to the Soviet Union despite the precarious future of perestroika and indeed Gorbachov himself, not to mention the salutary difficulties being endured by Yugoslavia where western banking aid to an earlier communist perestroika seems to have come spectacularly unstuck, should make the West think carefully.

The question is why has Mrs Thatcher taken up arms on this issue at this particular moment, that is apart from the obvious one of replying to Jacques Delors and launching a Euro-parliamentary campaign in good time? Much of the process of centralisation has been achieved by stealth. Even the Graziani Report admits that powers transferred to the EEC by national parliaments so far under 1992 procedures are exercised largely by the Council of Ministers which adopts laws *in camera*. Those committed to building an integrated Europe find it much better to proceed this way and as M. Delors disarmingly claimed after Bruges, the process of integration is already well advanced, indeed irrevocably so he would claim. Along comes Mrs Thatcher and declaims that much of this is *not* inevitable and that there are alternative visions of Europe. When she is compared with the late President de Gaulle she glows. Did he not hold fervently to his concept of the *Europe des Patries?*

Above all it appears that Mrs Thatcher is seeking to introduce her own glasnost in terms of an opening up of debate in order that perestroika, or the restructuring of the theology of European unity can take place. The Soviet analogy is more valid than might first appear. It is certainly more valid than comparisons with the United States. Like Western Europe, and unlike the United States, the Soviet Union is comprised of many diverse nationalities concentrated for the most part in particular locations for many hundreds of years. It is the greatest irony that at a time when the Soviet Union, having learnt that centralisation has proved a curse, is attempting, falteringly, to loosen up the political and economic structures, the Community seems bent on creating a series of centralised instruments of control. This also at a time when in the United States the Reagan Administration deliberately transferred power from the federal government to the states.

Yet the tendency of European federalists to make historical comparisons with the formation experience of the United States persists. When it is implied that there are much the same ingredients and that the outcome, i.e. a democratic federation, can be more or less assumed, it is misleading. Two hundred years ago there were thirteen relatively young colonies, many with stronger links with Europe than with each other, thanks largely to the Navigation Acts. Their total population was not much more than three million (compared with the Community's 320 million) sparsely sprinkled along a 1,000 mile Atlantic seaboard. To fight a war of independence they had no choice but to pool their efforts and resources. Subsequently, to come together in a democratic union made sense in political, strategic and economic terms. The land was vast, the people lilliputian by comparison. It was a question of sheer survival.

In retrospect it is ironic that it was the attempt by George III to tighten up the system to make it more accountable to the centre in London that precipitated the end of the Anglo-American empire. George III and his ministers notably neglected the fact that the colonists had enjoyed a degree of liberty for so long they were not prepared to see it diminished in any way. It is the gut feeling that the British people feel much the same way today that gives the Prime Minister confidence in her campaign to resist any diminution of parliamentary and economic freedom.

The truth is that the foundation of the American republic came at the right moment in history to create such a federation, one preserved at great price in the Civil War less than one hundred years later. Most twentieth century attempts to create new federations have been unsuccessful. Indeed, the elasticity that is embedded in the US Constitution was possible because it was bringing together relatively young democratic societies. Europe has no such advantage. The fundamental question rests. Is Mrs. Thatcher's Europe realisable? Based on the concept of pragmatic, step by step collaboration its main goals stand a much better chance of realisation than the integrationists who choose to ignore the fact that national loyalties are unlikely to wither in an age of transnational rather than regional commerce and defence.

One of the great tragedies of the French Revolution was that it snuffed out the flame of liberal economic thought in France (epitomised by Turgot) giving birth to a tradition of *dirigisme* which still pervades the Commission and its vision of a future Europe. Not since de Gaulle have the integrationists been so strongly challenged. The debate has just begun. As Mrs. Thatcher's forays in Europe have repeatedly reminded us, democracy is a rude art. Arrayed against it is an alliance of politicians, businessmen and officials who know they can only achieve their ends by maintaining discretion. The most immediate and obvious threat to Thatcher's Europe is the virtual stampede to offer commercial credits to Moscow. Apart from the distinct possibility that the European taxpayer will pick up the tab, eventually, it will create an obvious pressure for a detailed Community common policy toward the East. Bit by bit the pressure for political and economic union will intensify as an indispensable foundation for formulating foreign policy. That will certainly be the argument of Chancellor Kohl and his fellow Christian Democrat prime ministers. It remains to be seen whether, in the words of M. Delors on the process of abolishing physical, technical and fiscal frontiers between the Community member states, and integration generally, 'we are almost on the threshold of the irreversible'.

11

Beyond Götterdämmerung – Europe's Preparation for the Twenty-first Century

Noriko Hama, 1994.

Noriko Hama was Resident Economist and Chief Representative of the Mitsubishi Research Institute in London. She is author of **Disintegrating Europe** *and a frequent commentator for radio and television.*

FATTA l 'italia, dobbiamofare gli italiani. (Having made Italy, we must now make Italians). Thus spoke Massimo Taparelli d'Azeglio as the unified Italian state came into being in 1861. So might have Jacques Delors spoken of his European Construction, had it not been for the fact that as the Maastricht Treaty finally took effect on 1 November 1993, he cannot have been over-confident of actually having made Europe in the first place. As for the making of Europeans, it must surely be a feat that requires all the centripetal magnetism of a modern-day Vittorio Emanuele combined with the strongest and most incontestable of tangible benefits that lends legitimacy to the formulation of an integrated economic entity.

To this writer's alien eye, both such factors appear conspicuously absent in the Europe of today. The crisis of identity appears as profound as never before, at least in the past near half-a-century of the post war period. A customary retort to such a statement is that the wide swings between Europessimism and Euroeuphoria have been a familiar feature of the saga of integration; given time, the pendulum would have soon worked its way back to the other end of the arc. Yet it has to be asked if the European Community, or the European Union as it would now have us call it, has ever encountered such a fundamental transformation in the stage upon which it performs, as it faces today. Not only is the set design different with the Iron Curtain no longer a part of the scenery. However one of the principal players has undergone a radical change of character, from a rich and politically silent West Germany into an economically troubled and increasingly politically aware if not ambitious unified Germany. To all intents and purposes it is an altogether different show that the Community now finds itself engaged in.

In the twilight of the twentieth century the gods who envisioned the Valhalla of integrated Europe and their reasoning appear to be losing their contemporary relevance. Surely the new century calls for a new edifice, shaped not by the gods whose powers were destined to wane as the world grew out of its Cold War framework and began to sail in untested waters.

Four questions would seem to need addressing, if one tries to look beyond the plight of the gods of the twentieth century in quest of a new lease of life for Europe. One is the issue of economic viability: will closer integration remain the key that will continue to open doors to greater and lasting prosperity for the people of Europe in the twenty-first century? Second and co-relatedly, how feasible is it for the Europe of today to retain the goal of monetary union with all the requirements of cohesiveness and convergence that this entails? Third. Is it the pull of economic gain or the logic of politics and international relations which takes fundamental precedence as a motive for closer union among peoples. Was Walter Hallstein, first president of the EEC

Commission, revealing the ultimate wisdom when he remarked that "the Community's business is not business but politics"? The fourth and last, although most certainly not least of the issues concerns the rising internal tide of regionalism within the Community. *Secessione,* cries Umberto Bossi in the foothills of the Italian Alps. The Walloons and Flemings ponder the prospect of a complete separation now that Belgium has officially become a federal state rather than a unified kingdom. The Catalan cry for greater autonomy grows stronger by the day. The paradoxical outcome of German unification has been the even greater self-awareness of what were already considerably independent-minded *länder.* While the aspiration of regional entities within states to establish for themselves a separate political, economic, social and cultural identity has been a feature of European history over very many centuries, the voice of separatism seems to have acquired a new prominence as we approach the turn of this particular century.

This has as much to do with the prosaic issue of money as with the virtuous passion for independence. In the midst of the worst Europe-wide recession since the 1930s, Flanders wonders why it must subsidize Wallonia out of the pockets of its citizens. Northern Italy would like to keep its wealth for itself, rather than see it squandered away by its spendthrift and corrupt brethren of the Mezzogiorno. Industrious Catalonia feels entitled to invest the fruits of its efforts for its own benefit, not in support of infrastructure building in the poorer south. Income transfer via the state is all very well at times of expanding overall wealth; when the pie stops growing, the willingness to share becomes distinctly limited. The yearning for selfdetermination becomes all the more urgent in adverse economic circumstances.

Another form of resistance against central control can be seen in the case of Denmark's initial refusal to ratify the Maastricht Treaty. "If you can't join them, beat them", remarked then Danish Foreign Minister, and eminently quotable, Uffe Ellemann-Jensen on 26 June 1992, as he received news of Denmark's victory over Germany in the European football championship final. This was also the day on which the European Council met in Lisbon, three weeks after the Danish NO vote in the Maastricht referendum. As Mr Ellemann-Jensen's further comments the Danish team's achievement "shows small states can win". And as "Europe needs small states" implies, the underlying fear of falling under the dominance of the larger states, is a concern that can only grow as higher levels of political and economic integration are sought. And the desire to beat rather than join is surely magnified, as greater interdependence becomes the vehicle through which recessionary pressure is transmitted from state to state.

All this leads back to the first question of Europe's ability to generate growth. It would be stating the obvious to say that the current situation looks far from promising. The overwhelming concern of every member state at present is how to get its people back to work. With 18 million of them on the dole, that is a venture that needs some ingenuity. A Marshall Plan-like spending programme to construct "transEuropean" networks of roads, communication and energy supply, together with the call for a concerted effort to revive competitiveness through a better functioning labour market was the answer provided at the Brussels summit of December last year. Could this package be the answer to Europe's current woes?

"Growth, Competitiveness and Employment", the title of the much talked-of White Paper which introduces these ideas, is an apt one that indicates an accurate grasp of the problems to be tackled. Yet the solutions seem curiously out of step, if not out of date within the framework of late twentieth century Europe. The Marshall Plan worked so well for postwar Europe because of the presence of an immensely capital-abundant United States. It is very much open to question whether the Community's member states, each struggling with its own spending over-run problems, can collectively muster resources enough for the desired growth-enhancing effect without creating distortions elsewhere.

As for competitiveness, it is not a thing that can be planned and administered into existence. There is something inherently self-contradictory in the notion that states can get together and map out a course towards greater competitiveness. The achievement of higher competitiveness without lowering the level of social protection, and without falling prey to the potential threat to jobs that comes with the cost-cutting and productivity improvements required, is a Gordian Knot of quite considerable proportion.

Over and above these specific concerns, the single most problematic issue for today's Europe is that it can no longer count on the driving force of a West German locomotive to keep the growth momentum going. To the extent that supporting the Eastern side continues to drain Western Germany of its macroeconomic resilience, it cannot be relied on to play the erstwhile engine role for the Community as a whole. While the current recession will, as do all recessions, bottom out eventually, the longer-term ability of Germany to be the central axis around which the European growth machine rotates is questionable at best.

There was of course a time when the growth-effect of closer integration was indisputable. The years between 1958 and 1967 were precisely such a time, when the six original members of the Community benefited greatly through the mutual abolition of import tariffs and the adoption of common external tariffs in the process of creating a customs union. In so doing, the member states were able to break free of the growth constraints imposed on them by the limited size of their respective domestic markets. Together they enjoyed a golden era of export-led growth, which was impressive enough to make the Euro-wary British have second thoughts about their splendid isolation and make their first tentative move to join rather than beat the Continental team. This, as will be recalled, was in 1961. With middle-age setting in, today's Europe could hardly be expected to perform in the same manner.

Given these circumstances, the difficulties attached to aiming for a currency union at this point are almost self-evident. The current state of the Exchange Rate Mechanism of the European Monetary System is a graphic illustration of the underlying weakness of a regime of quasi-fixed parities which centres around a single national currency. Such a system is by nature unilaterally dependent on the economic soundness of the key currency state for survival. If anything goes wrong, either in terms of the underlying macroeconomic situation or faulty policy management, stability of the system itself is instantly undermined.

In this sense, the ERM and the effective dollar standard regime of the Bretton Woods System have precisely the same characteristics. The first-among-equals system of fixed exchange rates has been tested and seen to fail with the Bretton Woods experiment.

There was no reason to assume that the ERM would fare any better.

All the more reason, it would be argued, to move promptly towards a fully-fledged economic and monetary union. This the French seem determined to achieve, with their masochistic adherence to the *franc-fort* policy. Yet the experience of German currency union speaks volumes of the destructive effect of the premature adoption of a single currency between entities with differing levels of economic performance and divergent policy requirements. It may, moreover, be the Germans who decide to render the *franc-fort* meaningless by deciding to pursue a cheaper DM policy. However improbable the prospect of a Bundesbank which endorses such a policy, that is the only course which is compatible with Germany's growing preoccupation with exports as the key to the way out of recession.

Germany monetary unification was a typical case of placing greater priority on political considerations as opposed to economic reasoning. So too, essentially, is the *franc-fort* policy. Can a convincing case be made today that a European

Union is politically worth defending and nurturing at all economic cost? At the time of the 1948 Congress of Europe, it was indeed apt to say "My counsel to Europe can be given in a single word: 'Unite'" as did Winston Churchill in the Foreword to the proceedings of that meeting. Avoiding yet another disastrous war in Europe was certainly an overwhelmingly important enough aim to pursue through integration, even without the accompanying economic gains, had there not been any. Yet those days are long past, and the immediate postwar framework is no more. Important as it remains to prevent the outbreak of conflict, does the construction of a European Union have today the same legitimacy as a means to that end as it did in days gone by?

Twilight seems indeed to cast deep gloom on turn-of-the-century Europe. Yet there is hope still, for as Hegel would have us know, Minverva's owl of wisdom takes flight at dusk. It is in the demise of an era that the next age finds life. From Johann Simon Mayr, Gaetano Donizetti's mentor and whose Bavarian illuminati took the owl of wisdom as its symbol, to Karl Marx who questioned the existing system as none before him had done, those in search of a new time become fascinated by Minerva's messenger.

What form will that messenger take for today's Europe? The answer may just possibly lie in the resurgence of internal regionalism that was touched on earlier. By introducing the concept of subsidiarity into the Maastricht Treaty, Europe may have opened up something of a Pandora's Box. The official view is that subsidiarity only extends to states and does not apply to regions within states. But the representatives of those regions seem to pay no heed to such pronouncements. And indeed by setting up the Committee of Regions as an official Community institution, even the authors of Maastricht seem to acknowledge implicitly that subsidiarity cannot be kept exclusively in the "state versus Community" domain of conflict.

From the Pandora's Box of subsidiarity may emerge forces of radical separatism and fragmentation. Giving rein to such forces may lead to chaos. Yet chaos is a great deal more creative than struggling to maintain a stifling and outmoded status quo. The renewed prominence of the quest for regional identity is virtually the only totally unaccounted for development which has emerged in the time between the signing of the Treaty of Rome and today. Monetary union was already envisaged as an ultimate goal in the initial stages of the Community's travails, as indeed was political union. As such, they are already notions of a past era.

New ideas for a new age. It may be that existing states have simply become too large for healthy competition and as creators of greater wealth. If the European Construction can provide the stage on which these new and smaller regional performers are able to unleash their talents, the European drama of the twenty-first century may become a truly exciting one. On the other hand, if all that the Community can do is to cling to the Valhalla of Maastricht, built according to the basic architecture of the post-war framework, only endless night can lie beyond the twilight of the twentieth century.

12

Ideas about an 'Idea of Europe'

Richard Hoggart & Douglas Johnson, 1988.

Richard Hoggart is author of **Uses of Literacy**.
Douglas Johnson was Professor of French History at University College, London.

MICHAEL Ignatieff writes that when he first stepped on to Victoria station platform in London, as a Canadian boy of seven, he knew that he was in Europe. It smelled like Europe. This remark reminds one of an incident recounted by Harold Nicolson in his diary. In April 1936 he was invited to have lunch at the Soviet embassy, in its grim Victorian mansion in Kensington Palace Gardens. He, and several journalists from the *Daily Telegraph* were entertained by the Ambassador, Maisky, the first secretary Vinogradoff and the correspondent of *Pravda*. During the meal Nicolson felt that there was something terribly familiar about it. It was certainly not the Russia of his memory. Suddenly he realised that the Russians were playing at being Europeans, just as Kemal Ataturk used to play at being European. These Russians were really oriental.

Is it possible to feel, instinctively, as a young Canadian did, that one is in Europe, as opposed to other continents, or as a middle-aged diplomat did, that he was meeting with people who were only pretending to be Europeans, and that the Soviets had 'gone oriental' as he put it? This sort of question was one which preoccupied us and which we pursue in the book, *An Idea of Europe*.[1] But what was interesting was that for both authors (who have been friends for a great many years) the point of departure in this reflection was different. Richard Hoggart, having been a Professor of English and having created a Centre for Contemporary Cultural Studies at the University of Birmingham, found himself as Assistant Director-General of UNESCO, centred in Paris. As such, as a very English person, he found himself pitchforked into Europe. And more than that, as the representative of an organisation based in Europe, he was dealing with the cultural preoccupations of countries which were outside Europe. He was forced to reflect that many of the assumptions that Europeans have about culture and behaviour are not shared by those outside Europe. Watching a Moslem refusing to kill a troublesome insect; listening to an Indonesian explaining that he regarded his family as wealth; being a spectator at a village ceremony in the Pacific where unity was complete and where individualism was absent, he wondered about European values, their relevance and their power. This approach was personal, reflective, questioning (similar to the methods employed in his Reith lectures, published as *Only Connect*.[2]

Douglas Johnson, as a Professor of History, had been writing about the history of France, and about allied subjects, for many years. But whilst, like most academics, he thought in terms of being a specialist, dealing in monographs, like anyone who has to teach European history, he was attracted to the idea that one ought to think in terms of European development as a whole. It is obviously for practical reasons that most British universities teach 'British history' separately from 'European history', since students are able to deal with the former in greater detail. But the fact remains that one should try to interpret a whole block of

European history as a whole, rather than assume that the small communities, nations or national states are adequate themes for historical study. The history of such units is usually determined by circumstances which are external to them. Thus the two authors started from different viewpoints, the one personal, reflecting on cultural assumptions, the other professional, reflecting on the nature of history. But, like most Europeans, they shared a number of concerns. There was the relationship between the developed countries of Europe and the underdeveloped countries of the Third World, many of which had been their former colonies. The one author has wide personal experience of visiting these areas and of meeting many of their leaders. The other writes as an historian who remembers the post-war years when it was assumed that self-government for colonies would mean better government, that many fundamental changes such as the disappearance of tribalism would come about naturally, and that with aid from the rich states, the newly independent states would become prosperous. The fact that this has not come about poses questions which involve European responsibility. If the Sudan has been at war for every year of Sudanese independence except one, is this because of the unreal frontiers which European colonisers inflicted on this part of Africa? Has the political colonialism been replaced by a neocolonialism, so that economic exploitation still takes place, and Europeans invade Third World countries now with shoddy goods, expensive weapons and worthless amusements? Have some of the European values which independent rulers have taken over been misplaced and proved inimical to the proper development of these states, all of which have tried, in spite of their limited resources, to take on the trappings of a modern, national state? The conflicts which now exacerbate many new countries frequently owe their origins to the colonial period.

Then there is the problem of the holocaust. It has obviously been known for many years that the Nazis persecuted the

Jews and that they, and their allies, wreaked systematic violence against their political opponents and against minority groups, whether defined by ethnic or occupational characteristics. But it is only in recent years, and because of the power of the media and because of a number of spectacular trials and controversies, that the full extent of these atrocities has been realised. It is in the light of these understandings that one has to consider European values. European crimes of this nature are not, of course, confined to the Nazis or to their period in European history, but the story of the achievements of European civilisation, as contrasted to the savageries and violences of lesser cultures is now dramatically in need of revision.

Anyone who reflects on Europe today will obviously concern himself with the European Economic Community. If one is British there are all the problems attached to the British view of the Community, whether one is thinking about governments, political parties or public opinion.

There is a curious reluctance on the part of the British to think of themselves as 'Europeans' and an understandable reluctance to abandon the idea that ties between Britain and the United States are stronger than those between other European countries and the United States. It is not only the British who criticise the Community as a bureaucratic muddle, deriving prosperity from waste in a world of want. But it is widely recognised that the Community has reduced the xenophobic tendencies which have normally characterised western European national states. The special relationship that has grown up between France and Germany, countries which had fought three wars over a period of some seventy years, is a striking example of this. The problems of shared sovereignty, of rival economic interests, of establishing a viable budget, or organising a system of European defence, do not remove this achievement.

Within this Community, it is particularly interesting (especially as the population is ageing) to consider the role of the young, who seem to be less preoccupied with traditional, official, national policies, but more with human rights, minority interests, small groups, alternative approaches, whether they be regional, environmental, ecological, anti-nuclear, or bound up with aid for the starving of the Third World. Just as certain Basque nationalists would deny that they were either French or Spanish, but would insist that they were Basques and European (as would other small nationalities), so these protest groups claim to be international, spreading across frontiers and oceans. Recently it has become clear that they have their counterparts in eastern Europe too.

Relations between western and eastern Europe are another subject of shared concern. At a time when western European countries were preparing to lose their overseas possessions, much of eastern Europe was lopped off from the west. It can be argued that, historically speaking, Eastern Europe differed from the west anyway, either because of an absence of antiquity, or because of geography, with eastern Europe far distanced from the Atlantic seaboard which became the starting point for the explorations and enterprises which galvanised the west and made it the privileged heartland which enjoyed the surpluses of a profitable economy. Outside this heartland was Russia, for whom western trade was unimportant, the Ottoman Empire which was seeking an empire of its own, and Asia, with which the west (such as the Portuguese) certainly traded but in such a way as to leave the region's structure unaffected. However, the histories of those states which were part of the Hapsburg Empire, or the history of Prussia or Poland, are all linked with the histories of the west. In spite of the existence of the iron curtain, many of the inhabitants of cities such as Prague, Budapest or Warsaw think of themselves as being European, comparable to the French or the Dutch or the Italians. Economics and politics may divide, but culture can unite. Russians, through a long tradition of creative writing, theatre, music, ballet and film-making, find themselves firmly within a western tradition for all that they did not share the experience of the Renaissance, the Reformation, the rise of an economically powerful middle class and the development of any form of political liberalism.

In the light of these shared concerns it was decided to examine Europe via some seven different themes. The first was that of fragility. Europe has always known invasions, and has always torn itself apart through internal wars. No-one ever succeeded in uniting Europe, not the Romans, not Charlemagne, not Napoleon, nor Hitler. (Indeed it has been argued that a turning point of European history was the failure of the Habsburg Charles V's attempt to establish a world empire, based upon his widespread European domination, since the great imperial bureaucracy which such an empire would have required would have absorbed and exhausted too many resources). If western enterprise succeeded because it arose from the competition of multiple politics, this competition always contained within itself inherent dangers, involving conflict, the impermanence of success, decline and fall.

The second theme was restlessness. Europe has for centuries been a continent of exits and entrances, comings and goings, immigration and emigrations. The greatest of all these movements was that associated with European exploration and imperialism, led by the Portuguese and the Spanish, but joined by the Dutch, the British and the French, and eventually by the Belgians, the Germans and the Italians. The most striking of present day movements are the influx into western Europe of immigrants from former colonies and workers (cosmetically called 'guest workers') from countries such as Turkey and Yugoslavia.

The third theme was that Europe was a contradictory continent. There is diversity: that of landscapes, languages, lifestyles, religions and nationalisms. There is also unity: that created by great rivers such as the Rhine and the Danube, the canals, railways, motor-ways and air services; that created by a shared work-ethic in industry, trade and finance; that created by a shared enthusiasm for science and technology; by the great forms of art, in painting, music and above all the novel.

A fourth theme is described as 'Pyramids and Plains', meaning by this the historical and continuing contrast between the hierarchies of power, whether seen in terms of the aristocracy, the churches, the upper bourgeosie, or the order-maintaining apparatus of the nation-states, and the long push towards democracy, equality and the recognition of individual worth. It is of course true that India, China and some of the preColumbian civilisations of Latin America had notable distinctions of class and caste. But the combination of constant class differentiations and a persistent desire to end these distinctions by establishing a different form of social management is a fundamental European trait, even if it is not unique. It fits in well with the fifth theme which is that of another contrast, between individual and community. Individualism is the hallmark of Protestantism, of liberalism, capitalism, the belief in progress; a sense of community is present in the nation-state, patriotism, and all the reforms which sought to alleviate the worst abuses of economic progress and which have established what we now call 'welfare'.

It is on account of these last-mentioned movements that western Europe bas become a more democratic, more level and more open continent than ever before. But at this time (and this was the sixth theme) Europe has become more powerless than ever before, dominated by two super-powers, threatened economically by Japan, discredited by the holocaust. In the sense that Europe has become marginal in its ability to be either a military or a spiritual force, Europe has become the 'over-arched continent'. Finally, and closely linked with this, there is the theme of Europe as an incoherent continent. Some would say that Europe has lost its sense of history, and has chosen to create artificial visions of the past (in a museum culture). Without a sense of history there is little sense of the future or of destiny, as Europeans fail to create significant intellectual movements and decay into a society dominated by consumerism, servicing and leisure. The challenge to the Community, as it is to some of the states outside, such as Austria, Hungary and Czechoslovakia, is to create an identity and to rediscover a destiny.

It is perhaps inevitable that 'an idea of Europe' should end with questions rather than with conclusions. It has been said that 'An Idea of Europe' is a brave title for a book (Christopher Tugendhat, in *Encounter*, December 1987). Perhaps the concept of Europe is too difficult to define, and even more difficult to expound. But it is essential to try. 'Europe', said Sireone Veil, 'is like the world's memory. Everything happened there, the worst and the best'.

References

1. *An Idea of Europe,* published by Chatto and Windus.
2. *Only Connect,* published by Chatto and Windus.

13

The Price of Union

David Howell, 1989.

Lord Howell was a British Cabinet Minister and Chairman of the House of Commons Select Committee on Foreign Affairs.

JEAN Monnet once told me that national politicians would have little contribution to make to the creation of a strong, democratic Europe. This would be done either by statesmen who could rise above national pressures or by industry, commerce and finance, where powerful and irreversible forces were at work which would drive the Europeans together to act in concert. His view is confirmed by today's events. Industry presses ahead, asking 'Why wait for 1992?'. The financial structures of Europe are becoming rapidly integrated. Central Bank Governors and monetary authorities are in daily contact and consultation. No single member of the Community could move nowadays on interest rates or other monetary measures without first co-ordinating with the rest. The transport structures of Europe are becoming physically linked and standardised in order to operate together. Industrial standards are being pushed into a common pattern by virtue of the simple fact that non-conformers are simply excluded from the market. That was the lesson of the famous example of windscreen thickness-es which the late Basil de Ferranti so tirelessly dragged to the attention of suspicious governments.

Against this background of what is actually happening, the choice between a federalist, United States of Europe and a Gaullist Europe of individual nations exists only on paper and in rhetoric. In practice, a far more subtle process is taking place all the time which is placing our nations in a new relationship. There is, it is true, an important debate to be conducted about the degree of central policy direction which this process requires. This was the political question raised by Mrs. Thatcher at Bruges. Do the rules need to be imposed centrally and supra-nationally, or should the separate partners be left to make their own choices, wise or unwise, and pay the penalties accordingly, leaving the centre in more of the traditional liberal 'night-watchman' supervisory role to see fair play? If one country wants to over-tax its whisky, and everyone floods else-where to buy the stuff, do we need boss figures in Brussels to bring us into line, or should national Parliaments seek their own salvation? My own preference is very strongly for the latter course, as far as it is practicable – that is, for the lightest possible burden of government and centralisation. The forces of integration are there and working anyway. We do not need more state masters to hurry them on. On the contrary, the proper role of both those elected to serve the people and of the law must surely be to moderate the process, to challenge and be suspicious, always to query whether harmonisation is really necessary, to protect and conserve individual and local and national differences and idiosyncracies – **and** of course to ensure that those with higher powers act within the law.

But the key question is: where we have actually got to in this process.

Which issues have really passed beyond the scope and limits of national sovereignty and can only be tackled multilat-erally? And which issues can be perfectly well decided, for better or worse, at national level or at still smaller and more intimate levels within each nation? This is the question, the clear analysis and explanation of which people are entitled to expect from their political leaders. It is no use at all, indeed it is a path of great danger, for national politicians to pretend to their electors that they are in control of events when they are not. Nowhere is this illustrated more clearly than in the financial and monetary fields. One step has led irrevocably to another. Thus, the industrialists have badgered the policy-makers to go for the single open market, including the market for financial services which in due course creates the unavoidable need for freedom of capital transactions and unlimited convertibility of European currencies. This in turn compels national banking authorities towards a strong convergence of monetary policies, whether the politicians like it or not. We are now seeing the Committee of Central Bank Governors co-ordinating areas of policy which many people still believe, and are *led to believe*, are under sovereign national control. Even the decisions to intervene against the dollar are being co-ordinated, although of course the UK authorities, with their currency outside the Exchange Rate Mechanism, tend to be dragged along behind, rather than leading from the front, in this area.

Whether the next development will be the formalisation of this committee system of European central bankers into some kind of Open Market Committee of Central Bank Governors, or even some kind of European Central Bank, I do not know. What I do know is that people have the right to know what is occurring, and why. And they have the right, as *well as the duty*, to debate whether and how they wish to keep this agglomeration of significant power over their lives under proper democratic and lawful supervision. These are rights which are clearly being denied to us at present. I hear no debate, and see no lead being taken in initiating one, on the vital matter of the constitutional status of these new power-holders. Are they to be independent, within broad constitutional limits agreed by parliaments – a sort of Bundesbank model on a larger, European scale? Or are they to be bound in under tight governmental control, as in the case of the Bank of England? Are they to be called regularly to account by elected assemblies? If so, is the European Parliament capable of doing the job? Or should our national Parliaments exert far more direct and effective control of these activities and exercises of power at the supra-national and multilateral levels? Or should we think our way past these questions, and past traditional constitutional models of sovereign control, and devise entirely novel ways of sharing sovereignty at the different levels now necessary for practical purposes?

These are not head-in-the clouds matters but hard practical questions about how we are to be represented in bodies and gatherings which take decisions directly affecting our lives. Of course, the answers to these questions will come neither easily nor quickly. But to pretend that they do not even exist is to practice a harsh deceit upon people. And when it gradually dawns that things are not as represented, that sovereign powers have been surrendered to higher bodies without a murmur or explanation or attempt to adapt the political structure to check them, we could see bitterness and anger being visited on those who have allowed this to happen.

So let our constitutionalists, lawyers and policy-makers now speak up. Let them explain where power now lies and how it is to be most wisely controlled. Let them replace pretence with candour and show how sovereignty – in both the monetary area and in others – can be sensibly and effectively shared in the new conditions for our self-protection, before we find that things have gone too far and it is lost entirely to others. Let us know, in short, the price of union.

There is still time for this kind of leadership to be given. Those who trust, the people who understand what is happening on the European and the global economic and financial stages should now ensure that this leadership is swiftly provided.

14

Europe of the Mind

Michael Ignatieff, 1988.

Michael Ignatieff is a Philosopher and Political Commentator.

IT is odd that so few British people consider themselves Europeans. When I first stepped onto Victoria Station platform, a Canadian boy of seven, I knew I was in Europe. It smelled like Europe: the coal smoke from the engine, the Woodbine between the porter's lips, the brown sugary tea in the station restaurant, and the chill London fog that made the pavements glisten and the taxi headlights dim yellow in the gloom. Now that I make my home here, the appeal of Britain remains that it is a European society where I can be at home in my native tongue; for me Britain is just one patch in Europe's quilt of cultures.

But the British keep on insisting they're no part of the European blanket. Britain was the first society in Europe where a property owning class of peasant individualists emerged; the first society to create a common law; the first to make the transition from absolutism to parliamentary democracy; and now the last society to struggle its way into the post-industrial future. Britain can never be European, I am told, because its history is exceptional.

All European nationalisms appeal to a sense of the exceptional character of their history, and all nationalisms are blinkered by provincial self-regard, but the British sense of exceptionalism takes some beating for sheer cussedness. Instead of exploring the possibility that what is worthy of pride in England is that it stands for values which are essentially European rather than peculiarly British – liberty, tolerance, reason, respect for rights and for human equality – the British pride themselves on collective worship of curious local customs, and on a habit of mind Sigmund Freud called 'the narcissism of minor differences' – the loving exaggeration of every vestigial British difference from the European pattern.

These differences – particularly of political culture – are less and less plausible as grounds for keeping aloof from Europe. During the 1940s and 50s, when Franco and Salazar were in their palaces and the French fourth republic tottered to its end, the British could be forgiven for wishing to give the Continentals lessons in democracy. But since the establishment of French political stability in the Fifth Republic and the passage of Greece, Portugal and Spain into the camp of the democracies, it is less plausible for the British to see their island as a paragon of political moderation on the edge of continental despotism and political hysteria. A society without a modern Bill of Rights or Freedom of Information Act has more to learn from Europe than its habits of self congratulation allow.

Between 1918 and 1960 it might have been plausible for the British to distinguish the civility and tolerance of its social life from the often fratricidal character of European social quarrels. But thirty years of economic crisis have limited the welfare state's capacity to conciliate social conflict; Britain is an altogether rougher and more combative society than it was a generation ago. In many ways this is a good thing; since civility depends too much on deference – but in any event, the new public culture of the Thatcher era, which makes private gain the all but exclusive means to public good, is appreciably closer to the German or American cultural pattern than ever before.

Despite these signs of convergence, most British people still distinguish their culture sharply from the European. But now the vocabulary of distinction is stood on its head. Instead of complacently enumerating all the things the British do better than the continentals, the British now focus neurotically on the uniqueness of their economic and social failure. In the language of invidious comparison which dominates so much public discourse, Britain has become more European, but in the worst possible way: in the unquestioned and often incorrect assumption that anything made by Bosch, Braun or Fiat must be better than anything by Austin, Hoover or GEC.

Envy is probably an inevitable phase in leaving behind an excess of imperial self-regard. Invidious comparison is a painful therapy of self-improvement. Societies that do not look enviously, even unhappily at the success of their neighbours are not struggling with their own limitations. Yet invidious comparison with the continent has aggravated rather than alleviated the root of the British disease which is provincial self-absorption. A generation of economic decline has produced an inwardly turned national debate marred by all the hallmarks of the depressive, especially the depressive's narcissism. The new British sense of being exceptional, i.e. exceptionally incompetent, is surely no improvement on its reverse image: that the Brits do everything better. The one is as parochial and inward-turned as the other.

Just as a depressive breaks the downward spiral by recognising that depression is not a unique personal failing so British society could do itself some good by recognising how many of its problems it shares with its European partners. Our common economic problems are symptoms of a deeper cultural anxiety. Since the war Europe has been recurrently haunted by the fear that history is passing it by. Behind Europe's resistance to decolonisation in the Fifties lay the fear that Europe might lose its place as the centre of world culture. In the 1980s, the spectre haunting European thought is the fear that the axis of world civilization is shifting from the North Atlantic to the Pacific rim. When economies shift, cultures follow. When Venice lost its empire, it became a museum. In one of his last interviews, Fernand Braudel, the great French historian of the shift of the axis of the European economy from the Mediterranean to Amsterdam, London and Hamburg, worried aloud that Europe would be turned into a museum culture by the emergence of Los Angeles, Taipei, Singapore, Hong Kong and Tokyo as the economic heart of the global economic order. Europe faces the fate it once visited on its own colonies: becoming an importer of culture and the hired hand of other people's technology. The economic competition with the Americans and with the Far East is ultimately a cultural competition and the worries that it awakens are essentially ones about national identity: do we work hard enough, do we still have the capacity to dare and to innovate, do we still have the national cohesion necessary for collective exercises of the cultural and economic imagination? It is in this European context that the British struggle to remain a viable economy assumes its real historical and cultural significance – this is why it is worth fighting for the economic life of this island: not so that Britain can remain the cosy 'old country' of American tourist brochures but so that it can join with Europe in defending the best that Europe stands for.

There is no reason to suppose that European societies cannot adapt to a world culture whose economic centre is beyond their borders. Europe's encounter with the cultural and economic penetration of America suggests how resilient and inventive the European response can be. Instead of being the source of European culture's dilution, American influence has been a key site of its renewal. The British working classes love of blues, country and western and Elvis Presley has produced the international cultural industry which is modern rock and roll. The French passion for American film not only produced *la nouvelle vague* in France but taught a generation of Americans from Scorsese to Coppola to see the achievement of the neglected masters – Ford, Hitchcock, Ray, Walsh – of their own cinema. The Italian affection for the Western produced the spaghetti western and the new German cinema – especially Wim Wenders' *American Friend* and *Paris, Texas* – combines a message of poignant envy of American energy and openness with a use of the medium which is unmistakeably European.

The question of what Britain does about its identity is thus a question about how Europe refuses the fate of a museum culture, by taking on the forms of a mass global culture and giving them that imprint which make British television serials, Benetton jumpers, BMW cars, Armani suits and Burberry raincoats a password for design and quality.

If Europe is known to the world for its best products, it can also make itself known again for the quality of its political culture. As the heartland of religious war and political fanaticism, Europe has learned all there is to know about the high moral cost of dogmatism. A pragmatic, sceptical and secular civic character or public temperament has emerged out of Europe's tragic encounter with its own fanaticism, religiosity and nationalist fervour. Having nearly destroyed itself with strong beliefs, the modern European temper now is the most non-ideological, the most sceptical, the least dogmatic on earth. There is no European society where the secular religion of success and the religion of fundamentalist Christianity enjoys the same centrality as in American culture. There is no European society – not even the Soviet stellites – that adheres to the creed of Communist salvation. That is perhaps why European societies are less merciless about failure, more tolerant of difference, more open to a world of ambiguity and uncertainty than either of the empires which hem them in on either side.

In a Third World convulsed by religious fundamentalism, there is something to be said for the defence of this European secular character: not in order to visit European condescension on those who *do* have passionate religious or political belief but in order to lend support to those in the Third World who know that their own painful experience of Europe's worst – racism, imperialism – need not oblige them to turn away from Europe's best: its traditions of tolerance, respect and equality.

None of this would need saying were it not that Europe is, in the words of Richard Hoggart and Douglas Johnson, a guilty continent, guilty about the contradiction between its 'civilizing' airs and the carnage at the heart of its history, guilty that its cultural pretensions bear less and less relation to its economic and political influence.

The most immediate source of this guilt was colonialism. It was inevitable in the struggle for decolonization that a generation of European intellectuals should have looked on these European values with a certain scorn. Hymns of praise to European liberty rather died on the lips in an era when French troops were torturing Algerian prisoners of war, when British troops were struggling with armed resistance in Kenya, Malaysia and Cyprus. Not surprisingly the best European intellectuals of the post war period saw it as their task to give comfort to movements of colonial resistance. There resulted in the fifties and sixties what the French have labelled '*Tiers-Mondism*', a fervent ideological embrace of the values and perspectives of colonial resistance movements and the new post-colonial states. When these new states failed to become democracies, failed to defend European standards of civil and political rights and degenerated either into corrupt bourgeois oligarchies or left-wing tyrannies, Europeans either hesitated to condemn them or justified their failings as evidence of the lingering scars of colonialism. The relativizing bias of cultural anthropology encouraged the tendency towards tolerant condescension on the part of European intellectuals. It was held to be unfair to judge tribal and ex-colonial states by the standards of political liberty applicable in Europe. It was forgotten that if colonial rule became indefensible, it became so because it contradicted the European values of freedom and self-determination. What Asian imperium ever taught its subject peoples the values with which to overthrow itself? European colonialism handed its subject peoples the intellectual arms which eventually were turned against itself. Yet if this was so, if the dream of colonial freedom was a dream won in colonial class-rooms, then those who took control of postcolonial states can be fairly criticised for failing to live up to the lessons they were supposed to have learned. By the early 1980s, it became apparent, as it should have been all along, that Europeans could both renounce the errors of their imperialist past and uphold the universality of European values, especially the idea of human rights. The post-war period of European self-hatred is properly over. We have entered a period in which it has become possible, once again, to speak up on behalf of that European watchword 'liberty'. There are some French intellectuals of the Left who exploit the traditions of European liberty in a blindly dogmatic denunciation of the Soviet empire; others on the Right who want to defend Europe as a preserve of white culture against the Third World cultures at Europe's gate. But the watchword of liberty – by liberty's very nature – cannot be turned into a slogan or a battle-cry: it is a word to live by, a word to judge one's own failings by.

This Europe of the mind, this Europe of liberty owes more for its re-discovery to the writers of the Eastern bloc, to men like Milan Kundera and Georgy Konrad, than anyone in Western Europe. They are the ones who have reminded us, if we had forgotten, that Dickens and Joyce and Shakespeare belong as much to Eastern Europe as they do to us; it is they who have made us aware of the mental shutters which prevent us from understanding that there is still one European culture from London to Warsaw, from Paris to Prague. This instinct lies behind the remarkable drawing together of Western and Eastern European intellectuals: the support in the West for the

Charter 77 dissidents in Czechoslovakia, the Praxis meetings between East and West in Dubrovnik, medical aid for Poland. The Western defense of human rights and freedom of expression in Eastern Europe is not just a defense of individuals: it is a defense of the unity of European culture itself.

As a result of these efforts to break down the Iron Curtain within the mind of Europe, there now exists a cultural Europe which runs from Dublin to Budapest. But it does not yet embrace Moscow or Leningrad. We would have to return to the decades before the First World War to recapture a Europe which included the Russian empire. In that last fevered decade of the Czarist regime, Moscow sugar barons collected Matisses and the painters, musicians and poets of Europe's most backward society ushered in European modernism. The Russian elite that was able to consider Baden Baden, Nice, Paris and Dresden as home was admittedly a tiny segment of the population, but nonetheless they were the first generation to resolve successfully the ancient question of whether Russia was an Asian or European nation. The elite which produced Scriabin, Stravinsky, Diaghilev, Kandinsky and Blok was both indubitably Russian and effortlessly European, and they were the last Russian generation to be so. The 70 years of the Soviet experiment re-dug a chasm between European and Russian culture, and it is this chasm that the artists and writers of the Gorbachev era are now gingerly taking their first leaps across. What is ultimately at stake in the Gorbachev reforms, from a cultural point of view, is the possibility that Russia will once again return to the European cultural heartland: not merely that its artists and writers will be able to work freely in the West, but that Soviet society will itself begin to subscribe again to the core values of European tolerance and liberty.

In Germany, in France, this emerging idea of a Europe from Vladivostock to Dublin is a fact of contemporary cultural perception. Britain may have joined the EEC in 1974 but it has yet to enter this Europe of the mind. Part of the blame for this must fall on the EEC itself. The Community process has confiscated the energy and commitment behind the cultural idea of Europe and turned the word Europe into a thought stopping bore, evoking only the grey round of ministerial meetings in concrete bunkers in Strasbourg and Brussels. The debate about Britain's role in Europe is not fundamentally about the Common Agricultural Policy, about what turn of the ratchet of national advantage can be applied to the negotiating process at the next ministerial meeting. It is a debate about what kind of identity Britain can make for itself in the re-discovery that it has been a European society all along. That debate has barely started.

15

The European Tapestry of Nations

Flora Lewis, 1989.

Flora Lewis was the **New York Times** *correspondent in Paris.*

THERE is such a thing as Europe, and it exists in a much broader sense than geography. But it cannot be described without examining its individual parts. There are so many ways to consider modern Europe and try to pin down its blend of constant shifts and deep continuities. When I reflected on the choice as I set out to write a book on Europe now, it struck me that the salient fact remains the dominance of nation-states, despite the many changes in their relations. Nation is still the organising unit, the building block for whatever larger groupings may be shaped, and diversity is still the essence of what we mean by European. But there is no way to consider either history or contemporary politics and culture without clear awareness of all the links and jumbles, the cross-currents and the layers of influence which make the idea of European a reality. There are many figures but they form a single, identifiable picture.

That is why I decided to call the book 'Europe: A Tapestry of Nations.' It's an ambivalent approach, as modern Europe is ambivalent, homogenised in many ways, faced with many of the same problems which necessarily elicit co-operative if not common answers, and still marked by strong and warmly cherished differences. The more the ways of the world cajole people or press them towards sameness, the more they cling to the pride of identity defined by nation. It is no longer tribalism. There have been too many conquests, too much migration, too much assimilation of all kinds of exchanges from food, to music, to computers, for the old idea of tribe to have meaning. Nor, in the west at least, is it defensive. That has been overcome only recently, after what has been called 'a thousand years of European civil war'. The great, historic achievement of Western Europe (itself a strictly politico-military concept) has been to end all thought or temptation of war between its nations, bringing a level of prosperity never known before.

That is a growing, cumulative achievement, imposing new needs and attitudes as it matures, exerting new magnetic attractions. But the idea, which certainly did exist in some minds after World War II, of a great, unified European power is still far beyond the horizon. It is being left to commerce, to technology, to make the myriad little stitches which are pulling the parts together without the painfully dramatic, indeed impossible, change of an attempt to start anew. Perhaps that is as well. Organic growth is healthier and more stable than political or social engineering. It can still provoke growing pains, but it brings something more satisfying and enduring.

This year marked the centennial of Jean Monnet's birth. He would have been his usual part-impatient, part-tolerant, part-stubbornly optimistic self if he were here to see where the European Community is now. His original purpose was to make another war between France and Germany impossible. That's already a success. His thesis was that only by creating institutions do people make sure future generations will digest the lessons of the past. He used to speak ruefully of his work during the First World War in devising a combined Franco-British purchasing agency and then at the League of Nations. He found ways to solve common problems, but he couldn't make the solutions last, and he concluded that was because they weren't embodied in living institutions. Now the institutions exist, not as coherent or effective as he hoped but sturdily rooted. He didn't draw blueprints, he sought to launch a process. He wouldn't be surprised to find it leading in unexpected directions.

Now, in the words of a French journalist interviewing European Commission President Jacques Delors, 'Isn't it a bit of a bastard, a bit of a free trade zone, a bit of a political construction?' Mr. Delors, who has become Margaret Thatcher's nemesis because she considers that he is pushing too hard for a more homogeneous community and showing too little attachment to separate nationhood, said that was true, but the mixture didn't bother him. He foresaw, around 1995, 'a coherent and effective whole with three levels of decision, the community level which would be the lightest, the national level, and sub-national regions, which will have to be strengthened'. What he would wish, said the chief spokesman of Brussels, 'is an entity of nations maintaining their national identities but exercising a part of their sovereignty together'.

Mr. Delors and Mrs. Thatcher represent the opposing views of what the Community should be, how much unity to seek. Mrs. Thatcher is against a common Central Bank and a common currency as an attack on the very cornerstone of sovereignty, the money power, and she derides the continental concept of 'a social space', certain common standards for social and labour legislation. But they aren't as far apart as they sound. 'What divides our countries is less important than what unites them', 'pluralist democracy, the kind of society, the cultural patrimony' Mr. Delors said. That is also true.

The capacity for accommodation, for correcting mistakes, is the greatest strength of democracy. Winston Churchill was right in noting its faults and failings, and he was right in perceiving that no other system can match democracy in this most essential task. It can encompass disagreement, difference, even conflict of interest in its embrace of equal dignity and respect for conciliation.

That is the way Western Europe is developing, and it is producing a virtuous circle. The search for political solutions, not proclaimed uniformity to reflect the will of the mightiest, has made Western Europe increasingly robust despite its penchant for bickering. And the success of the peoples of Western Europe has reinforced democracy, buttressing its homes and spreading its appeal.

The other major fact of modern Europe is partition. It has been eroding in a number of ways, but these are still breaches in the walls, not a crumbling of the barriers, by any means. Still, the trend is accelerating as the East takes stock of its failures. Underlying diversity is no less in the East than in the West, though it was masked by the Soviet attempt to make clones. Now it is asserting itself, not only in Eastern Europe but among the Soviet nationalities. There has been no basic conciliation as in the West. Hungary and Romania might be at war today, so deep and sharp are the grievances, were the Soviet superpower not prepared to quell a conflict. No border, even within Eastern Europe let alone those changed in the Soviets' favour after World War II, is without dispute.

The startling new development in the era of Mikhail Gorbachov is the way people in the east are coming to express their aspirations. They say what they seek is to be 'a normal country'. This is a euphemism. The words 'liberty', 'democracy', even 'socialism', have been debased by ideological gobbledygook in these lands and don't serve well to explain people's yearnings. But when you probe for what they do not yet dare or are no longer able to say, it comes out that they are talking about Western Europe. That is impressive, to have become the inspirational definition of normalcy two generations after the devastation of World War II, whether victor or vanquished.

The rise of nationalism in the East is evident. And yet, it may be misleading. Ask a Pole whether it is the Russians or the Communists he dislikes most. The answer is that they have become inseparable for him. It is the Russians who brought the system, within the Soviet Union and later within the bloc. There is resistance to both, and the opportunity of the moment may decide which way the expression tilts. There is a possibility that ethnic, political and economic demands have been mixed to the point where it doesn't matter a lot which one rings more loudly than the others. This seems to be the case in Yugoslavia.

The one assertion that these diverse people in the East all make in common is their desire to be recognised again as 'European'. They will tell you that they feel cut off from their birthright, not only as Czechs or Estonians, but as Europeans. Even some Russians say that. The national urge is not only to lay claim to what is unique, but also to lay claim to the much larger common heritage. Identity lies not only in the lonely sense of nationality, but in the sense of a family of nations who have shared much, who have much more to share.

In this way, with cautious western experiment and with eastern heartache, Europe is taking on new meaning as it draws on its tumultuous past. No terse definition can be adequate, nothing is standing still. But there is such a thing. It is making too much noise, busying itself in too many ways, creating too much to be an illusion. The parts can be clearly named, drawn on a map, described. But there is more than the sum.

16

Fresh Interest in European Civilization

C.A.O. van Nieuwenhuijze, 1989.

C.A.O. van Nieuwenhuijze was Emeritus Professor at the Institute of Social Studies in the Hague.

IN a Communication dated February 10, 1988, the European Commission proposed a cultural policy. This has no formal basis in either the European Treaty or the European Act. Rather it appears as a milestone in a necessary development. Earlier ventures into culture have been prompted by the co-operation with peoples of different culture: a cultural symposium (1983) of the Euro-Arab Dialogue, cultural provisions in the Lome-III convention (1984) with the ACP (Africa, Caribbean, Pacific) Countries. Currently the prospect of the internal market of *1992* is – whether in spite or on account of its economic overtones – prompting concern with European culture. It is no coincidence that at a commemoration in Brussels (November 1988), J. Chaban-Delmas has quoted Jean Monnet as saying, in effect, that had he to initiate the European Community again, he would start with culture rather than coal and steel. The authenticity of this quotation is said to be uncertain; the fact that it circulates nonetheless, perhaps as a myth, is significant.

The Commission and the average person are similar in that to both culture normally is like water to the fish. Awareness in this regard will be raised only by specific events, such as the encounter with persons of foreign culture, or important developments, seen as cultural, which may cause some embarrassment. Accounting for culture takes an unusual effort of objectification and relativization. Besides, the nature and effect of cultural awareness depend on what triggers it.

In proposing its cultural policy, the Commission presents an argument in three moves. It tacitly postulates that the conduct of a cultural policy, political-bureaucratic as usual, is appropriate to the European Communities. It demands a thorough discussion of the present state of European civilization. Anticipating the outcome it proposes elements of a cultural policy. These items provide a convenient outline for this paper. It will address the need for a debate on core issues today and subsequently the matter of cultural policy.

It is neither easy nor customary to consider the basics of European civilization. The attempt to define it runs into difficulties about territory and substance.

Geographical definition poses three problems. The distinction between European and Western civilization begs the question as to differences, perhaps of shading, yet significant. The tripartition of Europe into the European Communities, the Eastern Bloc and countries belonging to neither appears, particularly to non-Europeans, as a cultural riddle. Thirdly, the role of national cultures – subcultures in a European perspective – as collective identities: to a European viewpoint they are complications; to a national one, European civilization seems remote, perhaps threatening.

Substantive definition is hindered by the lack of discernment between two meanings of 'culture'. One is comprehensive: culture is the frame of reference for collective and individual existence; the other is segmentary: culture stands alongside economy, polity, technology, and so forth. It is the icing on the cake of life: the arts, museums, libraries, folklore. The notion is mostly used in its latter meaning, taking the former for granted. Few will bother about the underlying perceptions of reality and man, deemed unduly philosophical. This myopic posture will prove a liability when people become alerted to their civilization.

Such a situation exists today. European civilization is facing major problems and its global role is unclear. The European Commission's demand for consideration of basics, albeit unusual, is valid and timely. Unfortunately the Commission fails to meet its own requirements. Its proposals are confined to the narrow, superficial concepts of culture. This prevents it from determining where the shoe really pinches. Actually its demand should raise three root issues: (i) the present and future significance of the European vision of reality and of man; (ii) its formative impact upon the European life-style, both as pattern and as practice; (iii) the implications of the current experience of change surmounting stability. To regard the matter in this way is unusual, yet less abstruse than is commonly feared, and more practical. A few comments on each point:

(i). The perception of world and man has three roots: old-European pagan, Graeco-Roman also pagan, Christian. The first is largely ignored; the symbiosis of the others marks Europe since the Renaissance. It shapes the experience of reality, which, as in all civilizations, pivots on discernment. Man, an abstract category, stands in reality in such a way as to confront it, in an unequal relationship. He prevails as subject over object. Over time the outcome is the 'modern' phase of European/Western civilization (from the Industrial Revolution to the World Wars). It is the frame of reference of Europeans up to the present.

Its profile may be evoked by a few pregnant notions: humanism and secularism; domination, expansion, exploitation, jointly known as economism, i.e. the urge to achieve maximum returns out of relentless, systematic effort; unchecked ego – and ethnocentrism, i.e. conduct informed by the conviction that 'I'/'we' is the hub of the universe and its true yardstick. Throughout, man's supremacy implies the downgrading of fellow man, as part of the surroundings, to the status of object or instrument- an incongruity pointed out by Charles Dickens and many after him.

Concomitantly all truth is provisional, and yours not necessarily better than mine or vice versa. Rather than cynical relativism this is the yearning for a perfection forever beckoning below the horizon. Hence the demand for freedom of conscience and democracy, the belief in personal perfectibility and collective progress. The tacit consensus on these matters, inducing mutual respect, is the cornerstone of the civilization. It is forever imperilled by jacobinism, the multiform arrogance of those claiming to be right.

(ii). The ensuing pattern of conduct is marked by three salient features. – The field of tension between individualism and collectivism. Man is uppermost; still he cannot exist alone. Community, variously defined, exists for his survival. One type of community however, the state, threatens to dethrone him, by usurping his role as the dominant subject in regard of himself as the instrument object. This is perpetrated on the strength of its claim to be the supreme all-purpose community.

– Man's domination of his surroundings. Any resistance or obstacle is perceived as a challenge. No bounds are recognised to hold. This attitude has proven tenable thanks to technology as the product, rather than the impulse, of science. Intellectual induces practical domination of reality. – The necessity to expand. Systematic dominance and exploitation have a spatial dimension. Europe shares with other vigorous civilizations the urge to vindicate itself in challenging the world outside. It stands out by the greater success achieved. The European states, concerted in competition, have assembled mankind into a cohesion which, though as yet deficient, seems irreversible. Their attitude to the others has been ambiguous and hide-bound throughout, now decrying them as lazy natives, then admiring them as noble savages, and forever keeping them at arm's length. In itself this is not specifically European, but in European-imposed relations of inequality its effect sharpens.

(iii). The paradoxes of man and of truth mentioned under (i) result in a third, that of dynamism. The motive force of Europe and the West is restlessness due to lack of ultimate certainty. Dynamism is built in, and consequently perceived as a stable datum, a characteristic feature. European/Western man is Promethean. On the other hand, manifest change, being experienced as something else than built-in dynamism, is commonly taken to be the exception rather than the rule, limited rather than basic.

The current awareness of pervasive change upsets this paradoxical perception and entails a loss of bearings. The price for success achieved is, then, the recognition that dynamism equals destablization. What is wondrous is also ominous. It was part of the prevaling euphoria to ignore this aspect. Currently it is beginning to dawn due to adverse fall-out, causing some to announce a culture crisis. Alarmism apart, it appears that not all anchors of European/Western civilization are holding firm.

Symptoms abound. The global integration of mankind in a pattern of interaction in interdependence poses a vexed problem ever since the Eurocentric (eventually West-centred) pattern, a carry-over from colonialism, has run into trouble. The welfare state, alleged remedy to the detrimental fall-out from economism, raises more questions, both fundamental and practical, than it answers. Man's natural surroundings along with his resources seem about to succumb under his onslaught, depriving him of a base to exist on. Increasing control over the vital processes of plant, beast and man causes embarrassment on non-technical, notably moral, grounds. The arts – to return for once to the segmentary notion of culture – reflect the prevailing quandary.

The ethos of modern-Western man has carried him towards limits of an unprecedented kind, jeopardizing his survival. A phase of European civilization is demonstrably waning. In the transition, reconsideration will render better service than either alarmism or blinkers, the two common reactions.

With this backdrop in mind, what about cultural policy? A few caveats to begin with. The impact of human, whether personal or institutional, action upon culture does not amount to control. It does not transcend culture. No valid claim can be made for the state or a body such as the European Commission to play a privileged part. Granted, culture relates to collective identity, and this to vitality. There may well exist persons or agencies, initiatives or policies, capable of exerting some, perhaps beneficial, effect. Important questions remain open.

Another misunderstanding has it that culture is good, the nice section of existence, and hence deserves protection – by means, surely, of a cultural policy. Actually culture is beyond the divide between good and evil. Why are states so friendly toward it? The European state and culture have been mutually attuned during the modern phase, now outgoing. At any other place and time there exists a discrepancy between the prevailing civilization and the cultural framework that informs the allegedly universal 'modern' state. The self-maintenance of the state requires, then, that it emasculate culture by taking it in the segmentary sense only, and manipulates it as opium for the people.

Clearly, in matters of policy one must tread carefully. This said, two issues merit singling out. One is cultural diversity within Europe. The other is the common cultural ground underneath the multifarious crucial issues we are wont to address severally.

The divisive issue of 'l'Europe des patries' will bog us down until addressed with a view to the imminent future. This is fully possible. Mrs. Thatcher and others have, during the autumn of 1988, rekindled the fundamental debate. This needs to be pursued inventively, not just by politicians. Meanwhile, there is scope at the practical level, as some random examples will show.

– The multiplicity of European languages deserves to be tackled in a manner unimpeded by the nostalgia for Latin and the 'American example'. There must be ways to convert it into cultural wealth, by spreading effective plurilingualism to a significant number of Europeans.

National history images are building stones of collective identity. Teaching them is the way to integrate youth into society, thus to ensure continuity. Present conditions necessitate a widening of horizons and a broadening of views. A creative response is the reconsideration of established images. The experience gained at UNESCO and elsewhere, with history textbooks is encouraging.

– Outward-reaching activities need watching. Most European countries practice cultural projection, to former colonies and elsewhere. At the receiving end these assorted activities are bewildering. For example, the maintenance from outside of distinct French-speaking and English-speaking blocs in Africa hampers African development by its divisive effect. Mutual attunement of national presentations, supplemented by joint European projection, should be advantageous all around.

Another practical suggestion refers to the problems currently worrying experts and public alike. Some have been mentioned. The way they are identified and addressed, each stands alone, attracting its own 'clientele' of interested parties. There is no effective awareness of their common ground. This sectarian perception needs to be amended by the attempt to grasp their interrelatedness as instances of one culture pattern in trouble. Until this happens everyone will wear blinkers and achieve inadequate results.

The moot question is who will lead. The state apparatus has limited calling here, not just because it fears to rock the boat. Academies and universities are preoccupied in other directions. The big foundations having routinized their charisma, the link between wealth and vision is again obscure. The media have little use for basic issues. Altogether, a challenge awaiting takers. Is there a role for the European Commission, reservations expressed notwithstanding?

European civilization and the constitutional pattern of Europe are both in transition. The cultural pattern and the constitutional structure of the next phase, neither of them clear at this time, will have to be mutually attuned. To the Commission this is a crucial consideration. The fact that it cannot take charge does not mean that it should make do with inconsequential cultural activities. It needs to express its ineluctable involvement constructively. If the initial expression cannot be more than providing occasion for, perhaps triggering, the discussion it has rightly demanded, so be it. In this light, the abortion of the initiative for a European cultural foundation, which could have become a move in this direction, should be no more than a temporary set-back. If, by some miracle, a European Academy came into being, consisting of perspicacious minds (rather than champions of vested interests), its programme would be virtually ready and waiting to be implemented.

17

My Ten Most European Experiences

Cees Nooteboom, 1988.

Cees Nooteboom is a distinguished Dutch novelist.

JAMES Joyce in Trieste, Marcel Proust in Venice, Rilke in Muzot, Kundera in Paris, Couperus in Florence, Orwell in Catalonia, Diderot in Amsterdam, Seferis in London, Stendhal in Rome, Strindberg in Berlin: our discussion today is an age-old European discussion in which personal identity and national identity are sharpened against that of a different Europe; sharpened and measured. Every public discussion in the twentieth century is bound to be derivative, based on thousands of similar discussions of writers with themselves, writers with others, in the present and in the past.

When, at the end of last year, I was invited to an exploratory talk with Dominique Fernandez in the Maison Descartes – which is not in Amsterdam by chance – I happened to be reading Thomas Mann's diary for the year 1933. At that moment – it was the year of my birth – Mann is in Switzerland. He has exiled himself, is unable to return to his home and library, and writes lucidly and analytically about the tragic situation in his native country and the bitter dilemmas faced by those who have stayed behind. He also writes frightening passages about the similarity between the two totalitarian systems that are in force in Europe at that time, one of which still exists. They are passages that, fifty years later, one would rather not repeat at gatherings such as this, because of the climate of good will that reigns here. But what has actually changed?

In Germany, a great deal has changed, thank God, but in Europe, if we view the peninsula as a whole? Let us take Prague, a city a few hundred kilometres from Mann's Munich, the city of Kundera, the city where Vaclav Havel lives in internal exile, the city from which Ludvik Vaeulik, invited three months ago to a conference in Amsterdam similar to this one, replied that he was unable to attend. The police had con-fiscated his passport and he wrote that even if the conference were to take place in Prague he would still not be able to attend. He added: 'So here you already have a topic for discus-sion at your conference'.

These words were read out in Amsterdam and I repeat them here, because I believe they are also addressed to us. The last thing I wish to do is to perpetuate the sickening climate of the cold war that dominated my youth. But do I have a choice? Should we keep our mouths shut and behave as if nothing stood in the way of our ideas about Europe and as if part of the European intelligentsia were not severed from this same Europe? Perhaps the moment has come to abandon our too long resigned passivity and to pay particular attention to the ini-tiatives for which Günter Grass has pleaded so forcefully for some time and which will undoubtedly be put forward here.

Europe. In order to bring some clarity into my thoughts and my European affinities – it is the least I can do – I have drawn up a list of my ten most European experiences. These range, as they should, from the historical to the personal, from the dramatic to the hilarious, sentimental, anecdotal.

(1). 10 May 1940. I am six years old. Germany has invaded the
    Netherlands. We live close to a military airfield. Junkers,

Heinkels, Stukas. My father, who was killed in a bombing raid later in the war, has put an armchair on the balcony and watches. We see the red glow of burning Rotterdam in the distance. Later we watch the German army enter. Banners, and an endless column of men in grey. Banners, music. So that was what it looked like, history.

(2). I am 13, 14 years old. I am a boarder, being educated by monks, first Franciscans, then Augustinians. It is impossible to be more European than that. These orders are almost a millennium old, date from the Middle Ages, they teach me the languages that lie at the basis of our history, Latin and Greek. In addition we learn, as was customary in those days in the Netherlands, French, German and English. Because people's brains are smaller now than they were thirty years ago, today's children need to learn only one or two foreign languages, poor things. French is often the first victim of this reduction.

(3). I have been expelled from all my schools and go to France for the first time. Paris is the first ecstatic moment in my life, but I soon learn that ecstasy has to be paid for. Someone has advised me to buy a *carnet* of ten tickets for the metro, that is cheaper. When I descend into the catacombs – in a country lying six metres below sea level there were no such things – looking around in bewilderment, I come upon a Charon who clips all ten tickets at once. A blow to my poverty. The French of the Augustinian fathers is no match for this, but I try nevertheless. I don't understand his *'Fous le camp, petit con'*, but I get the point and I also realise that, in order to be allowed to be in this city, one must speak fluent French. I learn it from lorry drivers between Lille and St. Etienne, Pau and Nancy. There is no other solution as far as I know. I should have forgotten this incident, but as you see, I have not been able to.

(4). I hitch-hike, the most exemplary European lesson I have ever taught myself, all over Europe, as far north as Sweden and Norway, but only in Provence, in Arles, where are the Alyscamps, do I discover my true destination: the South, the Mediterranean. This has never changed since. Kindled by the love for a French girl and the book she gives me, *Le Mas Theotime* by Henri Bosco, I write, at the age of nineteen, a novel set partly in Provence, the story of a quest that goes all over Europe, a grail that is sought, found, and, of course, lost again.

(5). I arrive in Rome, where the pages of Tacitus and Ovid, conquered with so much effort, begin to come alive. I have been infected by the eternal and sometimes suspect nostalgia of the North for the South, which, in the barbaric form of today – my Spanish friends speak of the new barbarians of the North, the new Attilas – is interested only in the cheap sun and at the same time destroys an ancient land. In its nobler form it aspires to everything of which the sun is god, that which is Apollonian. A monk from the monastery where I went to school has become *sacrista* to Pope Pius XII. I have run out of money and ask for an audience. Now I become a European in the historical sense, for, preceded by a Swiss halberdier in a uniform designed by Michelangelo, I walk through the corridors of the Vatican lined with busts of Caesar, Seneca, Cicero and all my fathers, hear, in the red plush antichamber the voice of the courtier saying 'Ma si, Eminenza, si, si'. When the purple sails into the room I kneel and kiss the ring, and am given a thousand lire. The Vatican is also part of Europe.

(6). 1954. Spain. The first time. Later that country will become the lasting love of my life, but at that moment everything, language, people, landscape, seems to me a mysterious, dark reverse of Italy. Philip the Second against Casanova, Zurbaran against Tiepolo, the ascetic plateau of the *meseta* against the loveliness of Umbria. We have, after all, a European pantheon to make our meaning clear. I see a mass celebrated by a Jesuit before the Blue Division which has fought at the Eastern Front, steel helmets, iron crosses, black shirts, and I no longer understand anything. In the following years, with an improved knowledge of the language, I will also begin to comprehend the nuances of dictatorship, censorship and exile. Another thing I have learnt from these black years for Spain is that some situations need not be hopeless and that some peoples can conquer their fate.

(7). Budapest 1956. I went there at the first news. The odour of gunpowder, that curious scorching smell. The corpses of secret policemen with money in theft mouths, people spitting on them. The ever repeated question: 'When will you come and help us?' All this is unforgettable, a lasting shame. On my return, the Dutch PEN club proposes to expel the Dutch communist writers. I am against this and leave the PEN club. But Budapest has marked my political thinking for ever. I am twenty-three, I write my first journalistic article, which ends: 'Russians go home'. They haven't done so.

(8). 1957. I have enlisted as a sailor and travel to the Caribbean and to South America, where I shall find out what this extension of European colonisation means. Our last port of call is Lisbon, the farewell from Europe, the city of Pessoa, but also of the Dutch poet Slauerhoff, whom you don't know because you cannot read our language. Too bad for you. Lisbon, Amsterdam, Venice, dear capitals of vanished empires, lessons to London and Paris. Hegemony does not last for ever.

(9). Prague 1968. I am there – in Paris, and write a book about it in the form of a reportage. Rebellion in two rooms of what Mikhail Gorbachov calls 'the communal house of

Europe'. On two sides of the house something is being suppressed, buried, destroyed. Vaclav Havel, on his side of the house, talks about the stresses in a society that is not allowed to live in historicity. But how about us here? The legacy of '68 was on the one hand a complacent, anti-historical, disengaged generation which does not want a complicated life and seems to have abandoned the past for a fluid present without encumbrances, and on the other hand the embittered terrorist sects in France, in Italy, in Germany, whose aim was precisely to force themselves an entrance into history in order to hasten its course.

Number 10 I will spare you. It would have been an anthology: the election campaigns of Guy Mollet, Harold Wilson, Felipe Gonzalez, a pilgrimage to Santiago de Compostela, a visit by Khrushev to East Berlin, one of General de Gaulle's press conferences at the Elysee; strange material for a poet and in any case too much.

So this is my Europe, viewed from the periphery. In the summer I live on a Mediterranean island, surrounded by the heritage of the Catalan language. In the winter I live in the Netherlands, that exotic land fifty minutes by air from Paris but as unknown as the Amazon. Twenty million people speak our language, and very often those of others too. People know us rather badly, and have tidied us away in clichés that are unworthy of Europe. To some extent this is our own fault, because we have entrenched ourselves, more or less in silence, behind our water defences, a strange tribe whose members, according to some, always go to bed with a tulip in the hand and according to others eat fried drugs for breakfast, a country with an unknown literature that is only just beginning to be translated. Small, but said to be the greatest investor in absolute figures in the United States. Almost bilingual: 17 percent of the English book production is sold in the Netherlands. Criticised and maligned because of a number of libertarian principles we are reluctant to abandon, but also a remarkable experimental garden which greater nations would do well to take note of. And if I have any recipes for this Europe of ours they would be the following: that all those countries that ever belonged to it should still belong to it now; that the larger countries should learn from the smaller ones and from their history; that the usurious fares that hinder travel within Europe should be reduced; that the South should not copy the North in its pursuit of soulless modernity and that the North should look long and closely at the South and its tempo and traditions, and by the South I mean the real South, where everything worthwhile comes from.

18

Nigeria and Europe: not so distant cousins

Dele Oguntimoju, 2000.

Dele Oguntimoju is Director of Publicity for the Movement for National Reformation of Nigeria.

IN its *Leader* for the week ending 18 June, *The Economist* observed on Nigerians that "the name and the football team are about the only things that unite them". This appeared alongside the conclusion it had drawn from the evident voter apathy in the recent European elections, namely that nationhood is not something that can be imposed from on high.

I do not know whether *The Economist* intended a linkage between the Nigerian experience and the European experiment, but someone who is in no doubt about the parallels, and who is principally qualified to speak to the issue, is one Sir Peter Smithers who was the Parliamentary Private Secretary to the Minister of State and the Secretary of State in the Colonial Office from 1952-1959. He is also, as fate would have it, a former General Secretary to the Council of Europe.

The letter which is reproduced below from *The Times* is one that Sir Peter wrote in June last year following the sudden death of General Abacha in Nigeria:

Sir, During the negotiations for the independence of Nigeria the view of the Secretary of State at that time, with which I agreed, was that in Nigeria we should attempt to put together a large and powerful state with ample material resources, which would play a leading part in the affairs of the continent and the world. This was attractive but it involved forcing several different ethnic and cultural groups into a single political structure.

The negotiations were complex and very difficult, the chief problem as I remember relating, significantly, to the control of the police and the military.

In the retrospect of 40 years it is clear that this was a grave mistake which has cost many lives and will probably continue to do so. It would have been better to establish several smaller states in a free-trade area.

In exculpation it must be said that we did not then have the examples of the collapse of Yugoslavia and of the Soviet Union before our eyes. It should now be clear for all but the wilfully blind to see that it is extremely dangerous to force diverse racial and social entities into a single rigid structure such as that which is being built upon the foundation of the Maastricht treaty. Recent history suggests that it would be best to complete the development of the Common Market and to call a halt to political integration in Europe.

The connection that Sir Peter makes is more clearly grasped when the reader realises that "Nigeria" is not a nation in the classical sense of a people with a common origin, tradition and language: there is no language called "Nigerian". The word "Nigeria" is nothing more than a geographical expression that describes the amalgam of a large number of smaller nations to be found in the surrounds of the area of the River Niger (hence Nigeria) which were put together without regard to the historical integrity of the distinct cultures, borders and languages of these ancient nations.

This reality is normally obscured in popular commentary by references to these robust, proud and wholesome nations as "tribes". My people, the Yoruba, with their distinct language and traditions and of which there are close to 40 million, are no more a tribe of Nigeria than the English, who number 56 million, are a tribe of the UK.

Like the nations of Europe, the only thing the nations that make up Nigeria really had in common before their enforced political marriage was skin colour, geographical proximity and trade. The language of the Hausa, the Igbo and the Yoruba (to mention just the three largest of the constituent nations) are as distinct from each other as the language of the English, the French and the Germans within the similar expression Europe. In fact, while the nations of Europe can at least look to the Christian faith as providing a foundation for shared values, the nations of Nigeria had and still have no common faith (as *The Economist* has noted football is the nearest we have come): while the constituent nations in the South have embraced Christianity from the West, most in the North have embraced Islam from the East.

No effort has been spared by the supporters of ever closer union to get the people to abandon their culturally rich separate national identities in favour of the synthetic "Nigerian" identity: they have been cajoled, scolded, bribed and harassed to buy into this designer identity. Those who sing to the One Nigeria hymn sheet are rewarded while those who prefer the ideal of live and let live are sidelined and condemned as tribalists.

The need to promote the One Nigeria ideal has meant that competence has been forced to take a back seat to equal representation as the selection criteria for filling key posts in government. Similarly, critical economic/industrial policy decisions are taken not on pure commercial considerations but on the basis of the need to allow all regions to feel part of the family. Thus oil refineries are situated in the far North even though the crude oil to be refined is produced in the far South.

Rather than economic policy and development strategies being tailored to the unique resources and competitive strengths of the component nations (such as would allow the Igbo for example to capitalise on their flair for manufacturing), the different nations have been compelled to march to a "national" economic goose-step. Nothing highlights this push-me-pull-you quality of the Nigerian State more than the field of education. While the Christian half of the country has always placed great premium on formal education, the Moslem half has not. Rather than each side being allowed to live according to the priorities of its own people, the Moslem half (that has had political control of the country since independence) has imposed its own values by deprioritising education, as a result of which the once respected Universities of Ibadan, Lagos and Nsuka are now no better than sixth-form colleges. As well as deliberate under-funding of education, the motivation to pursue the highest standards in education has been undermined by positive discrimination legislation that operates against the Christian half.

Far from fostering a shared sense of identity, the result has been to create a welfare dependent mentality amongst certain of the nations which has given rise to feelings of resentment and contempt amongst those nations that have had to stand back to let others through. Not surprisingly many in the Christian parts have voted with their feet by setting up camp in the West.

The imperative of destroying the original national identities to make room for "the Nigerian" dictates that local governments cannot be trusted and there must be increasing centralisation of policy. In the immediate aftermath of independence from Britain in 1960, Nigeria had a parliamentary system of government with three strong regional governments (Northern Region for the predominantly Hausa territories; Western Region for the predominantly Yoruba territories; and Eastern Region for the predominantly Igbo areas). The Eastern Region's attempt to secede to form Biafra and the resultant civil war provided an excuse for increasing centralisation. Thus, while still wearing the tag of the "Federal Republic of Nigeria", the country is in fact a unitary and highly centralised state. Thus policies on education, health, the economy, taxation and industry are all centrally planned.

The Nigerian experience is that when different nations are placed into a single political structure, they become preoccupied with their relative internal positioning. Until such time, if ever, as a single identity emerges, their collective performance in relation to external competition will be a secondary concern to the constituent nations as they drag each other down into a state of uncompetitiveness. This is the nightmare that Nigerians have been enduring since independence. We have spent our time checkmating each other while more homogenous nations the world over have been pulling further and further ahead.

Given the experiences of the peoples of Nigeria, the nations of Europe are mistaken if they think political union will make them more competitive as a whole. The natural tendency will be for the larger nations to jostle for the leadership position so as to impose their values on the others. In the process the bigger nations who fancy their chances as top dogs will provide all sorts of inducements to the smaller nations, who are only interested in being looked after, in order to secure their support. The seeds of such sentiments were there to be seen in the haggling over the location of the European Central Bank.

At a political meeting in Oxford recently, I was fortunate to hear one of the speakers define democracy as a state of affairs where there is such a degree of homogeneity amongst the people that the minority are able to submit to the will of the majority. Former Conservative Party Leader William Hague said the same thing when he defined a nation as "a group of people who feel enough in common with one another to accept government from each other's hands".

I would venture to say that the vast majority of the British people have no experience of living or working with Germans just as the vast majority of the Yoruba in Nigeria have no experience of living or working with the Hausa. Indeed the Yoruba in Nigeria feel more at home in the Republic of Benin, where their fellow Yoruba who were cut off by the crude boundaries of Nigeria live, than they do in Abuja or Enugu. It is this reality that explains why the democratic experience in Nigerian elections, as in European elections, is a hollow one.

One consequence of such hollow democracies is that candidates and policies that would be unsaleable to the local electorate can be pushed through at the supranational level. The evidence is there to be seen in recent employment law emanating from Europe such as the Working Time Directive. It is also to be seen in the means by which General Olusegun Obasanjo came to become President of Nigeria even though his own people, the Yoruba, and even his townsmen, made it clear through the ballot box that they did not want him: he did not need their support because he was loyal to the One Nigeria cause.

The related problem arises from politicians rendering their account of their stewardship in some far away parliament. The void between trustees and the beneficiaries on whose behalf they act is the breeding ground for corrupt and inefficient practices. Because a man cannot steal from himself, when the governed and the government are in close proximity the chain of accountability is shorter and the scope for corruption is reduced. The problem arises as governors are given charge over larger and larger constituencies. As the chain of accountability becomes longer, and intermediaries are interposed, the opportunities for, at best, inefficient allocation of resources and, at worst, corrupt practices becomes greater.

If the political consequences of these synthetic meganations are as unappealing as I have suggested, what drives people towards them?

Part of the answer can be gleaned from Sir Peter Smithers' explanation that the motivation for forcing the diverse nations of Nigeria into a single political structure was to "create a large and powerful state with ample material resources" so as to be a global player. This is also part of the thinking underlying the drive to ever closer union in Europe.

What we often forget is that the priorities and values of the world of business are, more often than not diametrically contrary to our priorities as social creatures: while "social man" sees (and wants to see) the world in all its colours and variations, "business man" sees the world as one: a profit is, after all, a profit whether it is expressed in Pounds, Francs or Lira and profits are best maximised through standardisation combined with critical mass. The holy grail of business is a mass market, with one currency, one language and uniform laws.

It should therefore be no surprise that super-nations like Europe and Nigeria are driven by the consummate desire of the business community for standardised and larger markets. But while growth through mergers and acquisitions may be a valid strategy in the world of business, when you are dealing with man as a social animal, any growth strategy for the social unit which is anything but organic is destined to be demerged in the longer term.

The other group of sponsors of supra-national states are those politicians who cannot tolerate diversity. Under the guise of promoting the brotherhood of man, they are secretly bent on converting all heathens to their values, beliefs and way of life. For these people, there can only be peace on earth if we are all Christian, Moslem, or secular, depending on which camp they belong to.

By 1 October next year, Nigerians will have spent all of 40 years trying in vain, in King Canute like fashion, to beat back the sense of real national feeling that the constituent nations have within themselves. In our efforts to cast out the demon of cherishing the identities and values that our ancestors lived by, we have tried the British parliamentary system and the American presidential system; we have tried multiparty and two-party democracy; we have had no less than six constitutional reviews; from the three regions immediately after independence, we moved successively to four, to 12, to 19, to 21 to 30 and most recently to 36; the soldiers have had a go and the civilians have had a turn; we started with Balewa, and then there was Ironsi; Gowon followed him who was followed by Muhammed and then we had the first coming of Obasanjo; he handed over to Shagari who was shoved aside by Buhari and who in turn was elbowed out by Babangida who, making as if to pass to Shonekan, handed over to Abacha, who died in mysterious circumstances and enabled Abubakar to hold the fort until the second coming of Obasanjo.

All the time, effort and resource that has been spent trying to cheat nature through genetic modification of the human spirit could have been used so much more constructively if only we were prepared to embrace diversity by saying to each his own.

The first step towards resolving any problem is to understand the problem. I content myself with knowing that what goes up must one day come down: Nigeria will sooner rather than later have to come to terms with the experience of the Roman Empire, the British Empire, the Soviet Union and Yugoslavia. Nigerians will need help in doing so to ensure a soft landing.

19

European Thoughts from Aquitaine

Kenneth Leech Pearson, 1989.

Kenneth Leech Pearson has had a long and distinguished career internationally with the British Council.

ON a golden August evening in 1988 a group of English, Belgian and Danish friends met to attend an open-air spectacle during the 28th Festival of Saint-Cere. We gathered on the ramparts of the mediaeval fortress castle of Castelnau which dominates the confluence of the rivers Dordogne and Cere at the merging point of four regions of Roman Aquitania: Auvergne, Limousin, Perigord and Quercy.

The spectacle was based on a satirical comedy with a Spanish setting, written by a celebrated French playwright, translated and adapted (omitting some politically provocative scenes) by an Italian priest as a libretto for an Austrian freemason who immortalised the Italian text in sublime music. 'Dove sono i bei momenti di dolcezza e di piacer...'

The occasion, the setting and the opera were uniquely and internationally European. Other settings of comparable historical resonance in Europe – Edinburgh, Athens, Salzburg, Prague – could have produced similar overtones. Outside Europe, in

Sydney, Rio, New York or wherever else Mozart's 'Marriage of Figaro' is performed, our response would have been tinged with nostalgia; not for our native countries, since no element in the experience concerned them, but for our shared European cultural heritage.

An aim of this journal is 'to examine European culture'. European history illuminates that subject more clearly than most discussion about the EEC, which in this context is an irritant rather than an inspiration. As a previous article noted, the EEC 'has confiscated the energy and commitment behind the cultural idea of Europe'. An obsessive bureaucratic passion for book-keeping and uniformity has obscured the ideals of mutually beneficial co-operation and continental identity that seemed so self-evident in the immediate post-war years (Churchill's 'United States of Europe', 1946: Council of Europe, 1949). As Edmund Burke observed, 'the age of chivalry is gone. That of sophisters, economists and calculators has succeeded; and the glory of Europe is extinguished for ever'.

For ever is a long time, even if, as Burke said in 1775, 'the march of the human mind is slow'. Is there any inherent reason why the political and economic boundaries of Europe may not eventually expand to roughly the limits of the geographical area which has already acquired by historical evolution a cultural homogeneity that is most evident when regarded from the distance of an Asian or African culture?

Europe extends from Iceland to the Urals, from Spitzbergen to Cyprus. The parts that experienced long periods of external subjugation – Arabic in Iberia, Turkish in the Balkans – emerged with an enhanced sense of belonging to Europe. Considerable historical acknowledgement for the nurture of European identity is due to the Habsburg dynasty. The Habsburgs confronted the Turks but preferred marriages to wars, distinguished between unity and uniformity, and appreciated Mozart.

They were, of course, far from being democratic, in any sense of that shibboleth word which Europe has exported all over the globe. But it is worth recalling that the only country in the modern world apart from the USA that even claimed to be a democracy before the present century was the Swiss Confederation.

So democracy, however defined, is no touchstone. It was feudal, imperial and ecclesiastical organisation that produced throughout Europe the major visible works of man; including notably the centres of worship, education and scholarship that were rounded in the name of Christianity. There is no doubt: that Christianity has played as central a role in establishing and celebrating 'the glory of Europe' as Hinduism, Buddhism and Islam in other civilizations, but it is also worth recalling that until recent times Jewish contributors to that glory found it expedient or were constrained to profess the dominant faith (Disraeli, Mahler), whilst intolerance as pernicious as contemporary racism was rampant between dominant and divergent versions of that faith. Ecclesiastical supremacy in political and social affairs is as dead as the Inquisition and in any case Christianity cannot be claimed as specifically European, if only because Palestine is not in Europe. Saint Paul came from Tarsus in Turkey, and Saint Augustine from North Africa – two early outsiders assimilated into the multiracial Imperium that evolved to become a culture.

To return to Aquitaine: it became one of Charlemagne's domains and was in due course acquired through marriage by the Duke of Normandy who was crowned Henry II of England in 1154. The 'cultural idea of Europe', already present in the minds of mediaeval troubadours, pilgrims and crusaders, was a clear notion long before nation states existed. The anachronistic label of nationality is irrelevant to the European identity of say Copernicus or Erasmus, as indeed it was to Mozart, who referred to himself as German.

'Nation', like 'pays', originally signified simply a locality or region of origin. Nationality, meaning citizenship of a sovereign state, rapidly became tainted with militant nationalism – for which the English tend to blame Joan of Arc. Local patriotism and pride are different, deeprooted, and innocuous when not manipulated. American experience indicates how even forcibly transplanted roots can contribute to a cultural identity. Jazz is as indigenous as baseball.

To return to Europe by way of anecdote: Gonxha Bojaxhiu, otherwise known as Mother Teresa, received the Nobel Peace Prize in 1979. When the award was announced I was in Ohrid, Macedonia. Albania, not regarded as a friendly neighbour, was visible across the lake. My guide from Mother Teresa's birthplace Skopje, showed and excitedly translated an article in the local communist newspaper praising her Christian vocation in Calcutta and proudly claiming her as a Macedonian of Albanian origin, like himself. 'Our people have been honoured in Europe'.

The national animosities that devastated Europe and obscured its identity are relatively recent and encouragingly ephemeral. The small town of Beaulieu-sur-Dordogne has active civic, sporting and musical links with the similar township of Scheinfeld in Franconia, a province of Bavaria. At an initial meeting of interested groups in Beaulieu, the oldest speakers represented ex-prisoners of war and deportees. Their testimony of private exchange visits and family friendships cultivated over forty post-war years was decisive. When the Beaulieu band went to play in Scheinfeld, they were impressed by the majorettes but also by the war memorials, which made them realise that German villages were decimated in their fathers' time like French ones in their grandfathers' war.

> '*Large streams from little fountains flow,*
> *Tall oaks from little acorns grow.*'

Large streams can arouse fears of inundation. Governments, municipal authorities and citizens are distracted from supra-national concerns by traumas concerning racial minorities and immigrant populations. Minorities with distinctive cultures and languages are older than nations: Armenian, Basque, Breton, for example. But the new European minorities have a common characteristic, often expressed negatively: they are 'nonwhite'. This is the most recalcitrant aspect of ethnic origin, because it cannot be disguised. The cultural unity of the continent has hitherto rested on the historical fact, whether genetically justified or not, that its peoples could all be designated as 'white', with connotations of superiority in all European languages. That there are many shades of European white, and that some Asian ones are paler, can be verified by observation at any international airport. Alexandre Dumas was not the only European to have a black grandmother.

The new ethnic minorities of Europe present problems of national integration, specific to each country concerned, that remain to be faced and solved before a new revitalised sense of European cultural identity can be achieved. These problems are soluble in time. Honest information and education lead ultimately to comprehension. You do not need to be white to appreciate Mozart, or black to play jazz.

Like the Milky Way, the prospects for European cultural unity probably appear brighter and clearer when viewed from Aquitaine than from Brussels or Westminster.

20

Symposium on the Wider Europe and the Wider World

Enoch Powell, 1989.

Enoch Powell was a distinguished British politician and writer.

My View of the Common European Home

IT is by the great unforeseeables that the outcome of all our strivings is dominated. Those of us who consistently opposed a relationship between the United Kingdom and other European nations which would involve repudiation of the United Kingdom Parliament's exclusive control over legislation, taxation and government in Britain were always aware that the political and military balance of power on the continent of Europe was materially relevant to the fateful renunciation then being demanded from the British public.

As long ago as March 1971, during the Heath government's negotiations in Brussels, I said to an audience in Frankfurt am Main:

> 'There is a profound consideration which it would be disingenuous to pretend does not exist. So far as conflict between the countries of the Community is concerned, the sole prospect which causes apprehension is that of a re-creation of German power in Central Europe, however remote re-unification may

seem. If this occurred at all, it surely could not happen by the inclusion of East Germany – and perhaps other central European countries – in a politically united Western Europe: the resultant giant state would be too unwieldy and disparate to survive, or, too menacing to be tolerated, particularly by its neighbours on the East. The unexpressed intention must therefore be that the Community's existence would permanently exclude or prevent re-unification, and would be more likely to succeed if it included Britain.

'I dissent. In the first place, I do not believe West Germany in the Community can either forget or renounce re-unification. Without wishing to ignore any of the complexities and qualifications, it is simply not credible that a new unification of Western Europe will obliterate an older unity which has such powerful historical and geographical forces beneath it. It would not be made any more credible by the mere fact, that Britain belonged to that new West European unity.

'This does not mean that Britain belonging or not would be of no importance. In framing the new balance of power which would be necessary if this development was to take place without catastrophe, it seems to me that a Britain not indissolubly embodied politically in the adjacent continent would be useful, if not indispensable.'

When the negotiation had been completed, on the basis of which the House of Commons by a majority of eight was induced to assent to the Treaty of Brussels, I returned – at home this time, as it happened, at East Ham – to the same proposition:

'There are two alternative views: one is that the re-unification is ultimately inevitable and therefore ought to be contrived, when it does come, with the least possible danger, disturbance and alarm. The other is that re-unification ought forever to be prevented.

'I confess that this second view seems to me unsustainable, and that the currents of history are already flowing against it. A European Economic Community as a means of preventing

German reunification, and British membership as an added guarantee of that prevention, have little substance or probability. On the other hand, if Germany is to be re-unified, the most dangerous form of that re-unification would be the addition, if it could be imagined, of East Germany to a politically unified Western Europe, presenting to the East the spectacle and prospect of a huge power confronting and threatening it. This would be all the more so, if that politically united Western Europe already included the British Isles. It follows that, if Germany's future is the apprehended danger to the peace of Europe, that danger is not diminished but enhanced by the Community as an instrument of political unification, and that British entry would increase and not reduce the problem.

'So the golden dream dissolves. Subjected to serious analysis, the claim that political unification of Britain with Western Europe would purchase peace or a better chance of peace is not only not demonstrable; it is not probable. In fact, on balance, the opposite thesis would be easier to sustain. The advocates who seek to enlist upon their side the memory of past wars and the dread of future ones are, wittingly or unwittingly, trading upon a sentiment which is widespread and worthy but "has nothing to do with the case".'

Now in 1990, almost twenty years after the date of those two self-quotes, the face of Europe is changing with cinematographic suddenness. The re-unification of Germany, then a remote theoretical contingency, is being treated in Washington and in the chancelleries of Europe as a fait *accompli*, awaiting only the form in which it will be accomplished. But more, much more, than that is happening.

The future of still divided Germany is now set in the context of an Eastern Europe transforming itself from the satellites or component parts of the Soviet Union into independent nation states appealing for justification to their own national pasts. From the Baltic to the Black Sea the nation state, with independent representative institutions of self-government, is on the march. Those with a taste for analogies might see this emergent Europe as bearing a close resemblance to that which was given shape and – as it transpired – stability by the Peace of Vienna of 1815. Observing how a devastating Europe-wide war was terminated by that Peace, we catch our breath when we remember that a formal termination of the even more devastating Europe-wide war which Hitler's Germany made is still awaited.

At Vienna the outstanding parties were Czar Alexander's Russia and Castlereagh's Britain. Contemporary Russia through its modern Czar – I intend no impertinence by the expression – has been talking about Europe being its 'home', occasioning jocular jibes about the Soviet Union joining the European Community. What is then this European 'home' which Russia claims and which – with equal, perhaps greater, right – the emergent neutral nations of Central and Eastern Europe are claiming? The answer to that question could put us in the right way of thinking about the Community mis-called 'European', into which the European Economic Community that Britain joined in 1973 is trying to transform itself.

As we think about that, we notice that we are not the only pilgrims on the road. Moving in the same direction are unexpected companions, whose presence nevertheless gives us reassurance that we are not mistaken. The European bogeyman Jacques Delors billed himself to deliver at Bruges last autumn a counterblast to the historic speech there of the British Prime Minister in September 1988. But what did he choose to talk about? He talked about a Community of West and East Europe, about the emergent sovereign nation states of Central and Eastern Europe 'joining' the existing Community.

That was immensely significant: what they were recognised as potentially willing and welcome to join was certainly not a politically united Western Europe. We in Britain may have slumbrously reconciled ourselves to sharing the government of our country with Germans, Portuguese and Greeks.

The most fervid imagination rampant at Brussels can scarcely envisage that the Poles and the Hungarians intend to share the government of their respective countries with the British and the Italians, or to elect representatives to vote with those of the Western countries in a European Parliament. They have not disentangled themselves from one political bloc to rush headlong into the embraces of another, and that an alien one. They do not, it may be added, envisage either that they will be governed along with a re-united Germany, exceeding in human and economic resources any other single European state with the exception of whatever survives of the Soviet Union.

When these nations look westward with a re-awakening interest, 'joining Europe' means to them something quite different from political amalgamation, a common legislature, a common bureaucratic administration and a common currency. What it means to them resembles much more closely what was held out to the people of Britain eighteen, twenty and twenty-five years ago. It means not being excluded from the benefits and opportunities of freedom of trade, of capital movement and of human intercourse between their respective citizens. It means the opposite of being met at the frontier of the old Iron Curtain by a self-protective and insulated economic and political entity, whose frowning barrier they would otherwise be forced to scale.

I will go further and attribute the same intention to certain neutral European countries, by which I mean countries whose self-recognition as well as survival depends upon standing aloof from the political alignments in Europe but who look to freedom of trade with their neighbours in all directions as the natural compensation for the limitation of their inherited resources. I mean Austria; I mean Switzerland; I mean Finland; yes, and I mean the two nations of the Scandinavian peninsula, too. They also are European, and they also have been not unmoved observers of the re-awakening of the nation states in that Central and Eastern Europe to which they are incomparably nearer than we British. It is not accidental surely that recent numbers of this *Review* featured articles about two of those countries.

The stars in their courses are now at last bringing the European Community round to a conception of itself which accords with the retention (or recovery) by the United Kingdom of its constitutional identity as a parliamentarily self-governed nation, an identity which its people have never intentionally surrendered and upon which their political life is founded. The removal of barriers to mutual trade and intercourse to which Eastern and Central Europe and the neutral nations on the periphery are aspiring does not require the erection of a common system of legislation and government. It never did. That notion was always an aberration, and it now constitutes an obstacle to the sort of unity of which the new Europe is capable.

Agreement between nations not to impede the freedom of their own citizens to engage in trade and exchange with their neighbours will indeed demand from many European countries – more than from the United Kingdom, in fact – much alteration in their own laws and economic systems. Those alterations will be for them to make, if they so decide, in their own way and through their own institutions. Common compulsion is no more necessary for that than for implementing international agreements on – shall we say? – environmental or shipping matters, on extradition or on postal services.

It has been a commonplace much favoured by those who supported Britain's membership of a European Community on its way to turning into a political and economic unit, to say that poor old Britain, late as usual, 'missed the bus' when it allowed seventeen years to elapse after the Treaty of Rome before acceding to it. We are now in a position in Britain to enjoy the agreeable sensation of not merely being abreast of the times but having been among the first to point the way forward. The European Community as envisaged by Her Majesty's Government under Mrs. Thatcher as Prime Minister is in complete accord with the spirit of the movement that is transforming Europe from end to end. A lot of empty rhetoric about leading Europe was expended in the early 1970s to commend renunciation by the British Parliament of its legislative and political independence. Leadership has now come our way, with no such penalty attached to it. We ought not to allow President Mitterrand or Commissioner Delors to cheat or frighten us out of exercising it.

21

Perceiving the Uncomfortable Patterns

Enoch Powell, 1988.

THERE are recurrent moments in international affairs, when the pattern of relationships and alliances which has been prevalent is transformed into a new one. It is something similar to what happens when, by a sudden tap, the pieces in a kaleidoscope are reassembled to form a different shape. The moments recur at long intervals and are separated by periods during which the existing pattern comes to be venerated as if it were a dictate of the laws of nature.

There was one of these moments in the early years of this century, when Britain, France and Russia found their way to an understanding or *entente* in the face of the empires of Germany and Austro-Hungary, and when the old assumption of an inherent enmity between Britain and France evaporated. That assumption revived somewhat after 1918, only to be replaced in the late 1930's and the early 1940's by a renewed alignment in very different circumstances between Britain, France and Russia against the Axis powers of Nazi Germany and Fascist Italy. This in turn gave place at the end of the 1940's to a completely new and unprecedented pattern, the division between a Western Europe under the hegemony of the United States and an Eastern Europe under the hegemony of Soviet Russia.

The arrival of Mr. Gorbachov at Brize Norton in December 1987 signalised another profound re-arrangement, which is now taking place under our noses and which will leave little unchanged in international or, for that matter, in national – politics. We are witnessing the dissolution of that dual pattern of North Atlantic Alliance versus Warsaw Pact which anyone alive today under the age of 40 was born into regarding as only slightly less permanent than the solar system. In its place will re-appear, like some submerged landscape disclosed again when the floodwaters fall, an older pattern, which previous generations would have no difficulty in recognising.

A thing which has as yet no modern name but may provisionally be called Central Europe *(Mitteleuropa)* is beginning to be discerned. It is not, however, new but very old. Its old name is Holy Roman Empire, that amorphous but durable entity which we British, with our visible maritime boundaries and our native ideas of constitutional government, have always found so baffling. In response – or is the response the other way round?- Britain and Russia are starting to rediscover and explore the mutual interest of those on either side of Middle Europe in a counterbalance. If what I am describing appears remarkable, that is because no political party has yet discovered how its interests are served by displaying the current collapse of previous military assumptions in all its dramatic significance.

As recently as a year ago Britain was resting its defence upon the creed that the Soviets were restrained from conquering Western Europe including the British Isles only by fear that the United States might intervene with nuclear weapons of mass destruction, an intervention guaranteed by the presence in West Germany of a large American garrison. That creed now lies in ruins, though to admit the fact is too embarrassing for Her Majesty's Government and considered too dangerous electorally by their political opponents. Britain and the other nations of Western Europe agreed only a year or two ago to accept on their territory land-based American nuclear weapons as being the indispensable insurance that the United States would go nuclear to protect them. The same nations have now stood clapping their hands with polite approval while America promised Russia to scale down the means of attack upon Russia's heartland and to start by taking those very weapons away again. The theory of deterrence, upon which was based the American hegemony in the North Atlantic Alliance, has evaporated into thin air.

It is in consequence of this revolutionary change in perceptions that the new pattern in international relations and alliances is emerging. For Britain it will call into question not only the North Atlantic Alliance but membership of the European Community, which has recently been ever more candidly recognised as the political counterpart of that alliance. It was noticeable for instance, that at the biannual summit last December in Copenhagen the agenda included a 'review of European security'.

The eternal imperative of Britain's defence is to prevent the domination of the adjacent part of the European continent by a power capable from thence of presenting a threat to the British Isles. For Britain itself to form part of a permanent continental bloc in Western Europe was always a profound and unnatural contradiction of that imperative.

Britain's natural interest is a balance of power within which whatever developments are to take place in Central Europe will do so in circumstances least likely to endanger the safety of Britain. Historically the perceptions of the Russian state have suffered from an ego-centrism before which the British have no reason to apologise for their celebrated insular vision. We would however be mistaken if we imagine that the rulers of Russia are not pondering today with deep attention the changes in Europe which will follow when the icecap of the nuclear deterrence theory has thawed out. As they do so, they are likely to discern in the position and role of the United Kingdom a factor of potentially crucial significance for the peace of Europe and the safety of the Russian homeland.

22

The Official Version

Aidan Rankin, 2000.

Dr Aidan Rankin is Deputy Editor of **New European** *and the author of* **The Politics of the Forked Tongue: Authoritarian Liberalism**.

Keyword Politics

THE Argentine film *Historia Oficial* ("The Official Version"), directed by Luis Puenzo, won two awards at Cannes in 1985. It is a modern morality tale, in which Alicia, a history teacher and mother, searches for the truth about her country and her own family, against a background of crumbling dictatorship and defeat in war. Her husband, a successful businessman and collaborator with the Generals, bitterly disappoints his anarchist parents who had raised him in a tradition of idealism, integrity and heroic failure. They accuse him of prostituting his principles and selling his soul. He retorts: "The Spanish Civil War is over – and you have lost!". I was strangely reminded of this statement recently when listening to Mr Blair address the Labour Party conference. "The class war is over", he told us, although he was less forthcoming about the victors and the vanquished. The class war is over, but now the "struggle for equality" revolves around race and sex. Class politics are but another of the forces of conservatism, a conservatism of the left like German *Ostalgie* or the sudden vogue for "industrial archaeology". We are all middle-class now. The working-class, like the aristocracy, exist only in unwelcome, residual form. This, it seems, is New Britain's official version. Who will question it?

Not human rights activists, it seems. Recently, as a result of a newspaper article I wrote on Pakistan's military coup, I attended a human rights conference at Guildford Cathedral, organised by an alliance of denominations to mark the Universal Declaration's 50th anniversary. We were treated to four fine speakers. Ann Clwyd, the Labour MP and redoubtable campaigner for the world's dispossessed, was the most effective opposition spokeswoman anyone could wish for, lambasting her party's record on Indonesia. Gary Streeter, Shadow Development Secretary and active Evangelical, rooted concern for human rights in Christian responsibility and love of one's fellow man (or woman, as he was meticulously careful to add). Baroness Nicholson, the region's MEP, spoke stirringly of social justice, minority rights and modestly of her own outstanding charitable work. She is a loss for the Tories and one of the Liberal Democrats' greatest gains. Bruce Kent, the nuclear disarmament campaigner, had the guts to condemn the bombing of Serbia and was applauded for his pains. All speakers opposed racism and war, all spoke of rights for women (but not men), all spoke of friendship among nations and a vaguely considered ideal of social justice. Yet even in the context of right-based politics, the two words "working class" were absent from every speech.

That afternoon, there was a reversal of roles of a kind that would make our politics more amusing, were it to occur more often in the House of Commons. For in place of the local Conservative MP, I sat on a "Question and Answer" panel alongside parliamentary candidates from the Labour and

Liberal Democrat parties. The audience were thoughtful, perceptive and genuinely concerned about the world's problems. They were, nonetheless, surprised when I criticised the consumer society, expressed doubts about globalisation and pointed out that Fidel Castro was not all bad, because he had built hospitals and schools for his people. I suspect that the Member for Guildford would have said different things, had he been there. Unlike the Labour candidate, a bright, articulate woman with a promising future in her party, I mentioned the British working class and spoke of it as a positive force – both as a collection of individuals and a series of distinctive communities.

I claim no special insights here. Being the only non-professional politician on the panel, I had the luxury of being able to say exactly what I wished. What was noticeable, however, was that some members of the audience cared deeply about far-off countries, and their displaced people in our midst, yet for their fellow countrymen displayed an open hostility and contempt. Unless they belonged to a minority group, the indigenous poor were not there to be helped but to be berated as "racist", "xenophobic", "backward-looking". They must be educated, proclaimed an earnest Quaker lady who had previously inveighed against immigration officials who lacked formal qualifications. She said the same thing about people in Africa and Asia, the so-called "Third World", but her tone was different. For Third World peoples, education was a "key to empowerment", for our own working class it should be a means to repress beastliness. The spirit of missionary intolerance lives on, but now the savages are people of our own kind, not the colonised.

During my time at Survival International, which champions the threatened indigenous peoples of the world, I recall an occasion when a student volunteer proclaimed loftily that people in London's East End "don't take enough advantage of the multi-cultural society around them". When I suggested,

half-jokingly, that we should think of the East End's population as an indigenous people too, the response of my left-wing
colleagues combined bafflement and anger. Brainwashed with
left-liberalism, they were incapable of realising the irony of
their position. At the very same time as they campaigned for
the rights of Amazonian Indians, and defended their occasional eruptions into violence, they refused to try to understand
embattled cultures closer to home. Survival's literature frequently quotes a joint declaration by the Navajo, Sioux and
Iroquois peoples, issued in 1978 and, unlike the famous speech
of Chief Seattle, not a forgery:

*Our roots are deep in the land where we live. We have a great
love for our country, for our birthplace is here. The soil is rich from
the bones of thousands of our generations. Each of us was created
in these lands and it is our duty to take care of them, because from
these lands will spring the future of our peoples. We will walk
about with great respect for the Earth, for it is a very Sacred Place.*

Uttered by Native Americans, such sentiments are
laudable, an ideal blend of tribal consciousness and environmental friendliness. On European lips, they resemble at best
the late nineteenth century *volkisch* mysticism, at worst the
"blood and soil" ideology of Walther Darre, the Nazi
Agriculture Minister and proto-Green, according to some. The
ancient tribes of the Americas can talk about rootedness, sense
of place and the uniqueness of their cultures. For Europeans,
especially poorer Europeans, to do so is fascistic, since – to
quote Mr Blair once more – "we are all internationalists now".

Britain's class war is far from over. It has merely been
thrown into reverse. Nowhere is this antagonism more
apparent than in the "anti-racist" movement. Watch any public
protest against racism and you will see middle-class students
and academics marching into areas of deprivation to clash with
alienated working-class youth. Forget transnational corpora-
tions, forget the City, forget railway fat cats and other more
obvious "enemies of the people". For the information rich, *bien*

pensant left-wingers of New Britain, the real class enemy are the white urban poor, because they hold, or have the potential to hold, racist opinions. Such leftists make hollow concessions to socialism's working-class roots. They affect bad cockney accents, which fool no one, or dress in designer grunge which members of the real working class would be ashamed to wear. One new leftist of my acquaintance let his stockbroker father buy him a car, but made sure it was a red Ford Escort so that he could "identify with the masses". Naturally, he drove it to anti-racist protests, going to places in London he had never visited before and would have no reason ever to visit again. Ironically, this kind of left-wing protest is a form of co-operation with authority and not a rebellion against it. The state, after all, is "anti-racist", with a growing nationalised industry of bureaucrats to tackle existing discrimination and unearth it in new forms. Liberal journalists, social workers and worthy human rights activists alike regard "eliminating racism" as more important than abolishing poverty or repairing communities fractured by unemployment, drugs and family breakdown. In the official version of race relations, the line between sounding off in the pub about immigrants and a denial that the Holocaust ever happened is breaking down fast. We are losing the sense of proportion that once characterised us as a people.

"One Nation Toryism" was a phrase often on my lips in the Guildford Cathedral talk. This was intended first to draw a distinction between true conservatism and the dogmas of neo-liberal economics in which the present day Toryism is imprisoned. The second intention was to remind the audience that we are a nation of individual citizens with obligations towards each other that transcend loyalties to race, sex, religion (or lack thereof) and even, perhaps especially, class. When Disraeli defined "the betterment of the condition of the people" as the aim of Tory reform, his intention was to unite all sections of society in a common programme of betterment, to rise above social division by constructive engagement between classes, rather than by pretending that certain classes do not exist. So defined, One Nation Toryism is more than a conservative political doctrine. It offers a liberal vision of humanity, based on the value of the individual, his place in a wider national community and his obligation to other individuals within that community. One of those obligations is tolerance. By contrast, the "rights-based" culture of the middle class left promotes conflict between narrow interest groups and herds individuals into those groups whether they wish to belong to them or not. It is clear already that in the elections for a London mayor next year the contenders will address as "black voters", "gay voters" or "youth", rather than as Londoners those who share the inheritance of a great civic culture.

In *The Authoritarian Personality*, that seminal study of the right-wing mentality, Theodor Adorno and his Frankfurt School colleagues distinguish between the genuine conservative, who values tradition, and the pseudo-conservative, who combines intolerance with a sadistic taste for power. Adorno's work was published in 1948, in the aftermath of Holocaust and War. In today's "politically correct" age, an updated version is required, one which distinguishes the true liberal from the pseudo-liberal. For the true liberal believes in opportunities for individuals of all backgrounds, acknowledges enriching differences of temperament and culture, views political problems as complex and various and values freedom of speech and freedom of thought. He strives for an equitable society, not a perfect society. The pseudo-liberal, by contrast, sees individuals only as ciphers for wider social questions. When he sees a black man, he does not see a living, breathing fellow human being with needs, desires and fears of his own. He sees an "issue", a "problem" or a series of abstract "rights". When he sees a white working man, he sees an ignorant bigot and a probable racist, instead of a fellow citizen. In this sense, the pseudo-liberal is rather like Dr Benway, the medical villain in William Burroughs's *Naked Lunch*, who refused to name the patient, but refers to him by his disease instead. The pseudo-liberal loathes the idea of an equitable society. He wants a socially engineered "equality" of everything except income. In his world, where the democratic and the demotic are wilfully confused, rock stars or football players are allowed to amass vast wealth because they represent the popular taste, but all hereditary privilege is by definition bad. The pseudo-liberal speaks eloquently of "multiculturalism", by which he means a levelled-down, standardised culture where peoples who have forgotten their past are fooled by populist politicians and controlled by business élites. Pseudo-liberalism is more insidious, in its own way, than its ancestor Stalinism, its purported enemy fascism and its tactical ally, capitalism in the raw. Unlike the authoritarian movements of the past, it uses the language of inclusion, equality and even reconciliation, but means the very opposite of all three.

That the *bien pensant* professional should view the working class as "racists" at all is evidence of the collapse of "One Nation" values, or the very idea of a national conversation. For a start, working class communities are and have always been culturally diverse. The student who criticised "East Enders" for not being multi-cultural enough was blissfully unaware of the waves of immigration that have shaped the East Enders of today, although he was a student of political science. Second, it is the working class communities since the Second World War that have made multi-culturalism in Britain such a success. It is true that there has been prejudice, aberrant actions and on occasion monstrous events that have rightly horrified the nation. Yet the larger picture has been a tolerance, integration and creative mixing of cultures that is unprecedented in modern Europe. The spirit of pragmatic tolerance in working-class neighbourhoods occurs in spite of, not because of, the politically correct thought police. It occurs, often enough, because majority and minority populations find common ground in resisting officialdom, or in defending conservative values against the growing "liberal dictatorship".

A few years ago, the words "liberal dictatorship" would have smacked of journalistic hyperbole. Today, the main threat to freedom comes less from the authoritarian right (although it still exists) than from those who once most stridently opposed censorship of all kinds. It is not, as yet, a direct threat to my freedom, or to that of most readers of this journal. Those who are threatened most are the information poor, who lack access to media and politics, whose lives are ever-more dominated by the missionaries of political correctness: social services, the agencies of local government and now, increasingly, the police. A case in point is Mr George Staunton, a former dock worker and Second World War veteran from Liverpool. Mr Staunton, an 84-year old, was arrested in mid-1999 for daubing the slogans "Free Speech for England" and "Remember 1939-1945" on an abandoned building. For this, he was charged with "racially aggravated" criminal damage, under laws passed by New Labour without much comment which increase the severity of sentencing whenever a racial motive can be perceived. That the wisdom of such laws has been so little questioned shows the parlous state to which British politics have sunk and the craven nature of our opposition parties. Be that as it may, Mr Staunton was saved from prosecution and probable imprisonment only because he was fortunate enough to have a solicitor who cared genuinely about civil rights and was willing to publicise the case at civic and national levels. How many more are less lucky? Such laws are framed by the middle class to trap the inarticulate and the poor of any race.

Mr Staunton's actions were eccentric, perhaps, but racially motivated they were clearly not. Throughout his ordeal, he protested his complete lack of racial prejudice, but failed to convince the Merseyside Police. His party, the UKIP, is neither racist nor xenophobic. It is opposed to British membership of the European Union and has members and supporters from ethnic minorities, many of whom are worried by the more genuine racism of continental politics. One would think from the propaganda of "anti-racists" (who are really racists in reverse) that British politics had produced a Haider, a Blocher or a Le Pen, when in reality no party of the extreme right or the extreme left has ever proved electorally competent. Most worrying of all is the idea that to remember the Second World War, or to advocate free speech is somehow an indication of racial prejudice. Such notions, born of a new form of Euro-fundamentalism, threaten our understanding of history and (as Mr Staunton writes) our birthright of freedom of speech.

At Survival International, I was made aware of the distinction between genocide, which is swift and bloody, and ethnocide, which is a war of cultural attrition, by which a people's identity is lost. I believe we might be witnessing a form of ethnocide within our working-class communities, affecting people of all racial and religious origins. It is ethnocide through "progressive education", which denies the value of historical memory, through the breakdown of family and community ties and through all forms of political correctness which stand in the way of critical thought. It is not just "anti-racism" that is disguised anti-working class propaganda. Much of the dislike of masculine values shown by the liberal élite is part of a wider hostility to working class culture. Firemen are "too macho", according to an official report. New Britain's opinion formers seem to celebrate homosexuality but perceive as a vice the comradeship of working men. Ethnocide is a process that severs a people from its past. It makes them malleable to commercialism or ripe for absorption in a larger, more remote political order.

Marx was wrong, a century and a half ago, when he told us that the workers have no country. Internationalism is the luxury of the rich, not the prerogative of the poor. The institutions of civil society and the symbols of nationhood are taken most seriously by those who lack economic power. The "official version" of politics tells us that global homogeneity and European political union are both inevitable. It tells us not to think in terms of shared values as a nation or people, but to combine an incoherent internationalism with the narrow group politics of race, sex, sexual orientation or age. It tells us that gross disparities of income are not inequality at all, but equality redefined, for we have no class any more, only a "meritocracy". It tells us that anyone who questions the inevitable is reactionary, xenophobic or, worst of all, a cultural conservative. The task of thoughtful political campaigners today should be to prove that official version wrong, to show that we can be a nation of robust individuals once again.

23

Europe, America and Asia

Geoffrey Rippon, 1989.

Lord Rippon negotiated Britain's entry to the European Economic Community and was Honorary President of the British Section of the European League for Economic Co-operation.

AS we move forward to the creation of the Single Market in services as well as goods by 1992 our thoughts have concentrated on what is happening inside the European Community. We are now opening up a wider debate on the longer-term future. In this regard Mrs. Thatcher's famous speech last year in Bruges has received close attention. It deserves to be read in full. It was neither negative nor nationalistic, and I believe it has been widely misinterpreted. She said of the British position quite unequivocally: 'Our destiny is in Europe as part of the Community. We have all signed the Single European Act and progress towards its implementation is now irreversible.'

Up to and beyond *1992* we will move forward step by step with realism towards an ever closer union of the peoples of Europe although not always entirely in unison. Sometimes Britain will appear faltering and lacking in commitment, as is the case for example with our continued failure, which I regret, to join the EMS regulatory system on the grounds that the time is not yet ripe for us to do so. Sometimes, however, Britain will be ahead as with freedom of capital movements, the abolition of exchange control and the issue of Ecu-denominated Treasury Bonds. We all have our views about how fast and how far we can proceed but in the process we must take note of what I regard as the essential message of Mrs. Thatcher's Bruges speech, namely that the European Community must not become inward-looking. It is not an end in itself.

First of all there are the countries of the Council of Europe and the members of the European Free Trade Area. They are also Europeans. So too are the peoples east of the Iron Curtain who once enjoyed a full share of European culture, freedom and identity. As Margaret Thatcher said: 'We shall always look on Warsaw, Prague and Budapest as great European cities'. Even the Russians now talk about a 'European Home'.

Secondly, we must all, I think, agree with Mrs. Thatcher that our common future does not lie only in Europe. There is a world beyond and we have to see our European future in the context of our global interests and responsibilities. In my view, close trading and political relations with America, Asia and the rest of the world are complementary and not contradictory to what we seek to achieve in our own continent. In both America and Asia fears have been expressed that we may be building a 'Fortress Europe'. I do not believe this to be so, if only because it is in nobody's interest and it has been well said that interest never lies. Currently trade between EEC countries and the outside world amounts on average to 24% of the Community's GDP compared with Japan's 23% and the USA's 14%. On the other side of the coin presently Europe attracts over 40% of total US investment and 19% of Japanese. There is almost 130 billion dollars of direct US investment in Europe. The US and Japanese banks and major companies are already established and others will enter the competitive fray before 1992. We must welcome them.

European industries and businesses will not only have to be more competitive vis-a-vis each other but will also face increasing international competition. US and Japanese investment is something I regard as desirable and is in effect a vote of confidence in Europe. We have to look for increased trade and so competition – with Hong Kong, Taiwan, Korea and other countries of Asia. We have to face that competition. If, indeed, we tried to erect a Fortress Europe we should all be its first prisoners. The creation of the Single Market should be seen as a first step towards greater trade liberalisation throughout the world. It would be wholly wrong to take down barriers within Europe but to retain them around our own larger market.

On the contrary the Community's policy must be to seek to reduce voluntary restriction agreements, to remove tariffs and quotas on imports from the developed countries, while seeking more open access to third country markets for Community exports. To that end we must be prepared to end barriers to inward investment such as 'local content' rules. Furthermore, we should use the Community's growing economic strength to negotiate bilateral and multilateral agreements to open up markets as a supplement to the current GATT negotiations. We should not only phase out existing restrictions and voluntary restraint agreements with third countries by 1992; we should also end the use of anti-dumping suits and similar protectionist devices. If we do so we will not only remove the fears that have been expressed in the United States, Japan, Asia and elsewhere, but we will be in a stronger position to insist on genuine reciprocity.

The meaning of the concept of 'reciprocity' is unclear to many people. The Japanese feel that it is targeted on them in a hostile fashion. As a general concept reciprocity is not unreasonable. It can, however, be used as a cover for protection. Strict section by section reciprocity sets up unrealistic standards and could be as easily applied against the Community as against any other economy. Certainly there is a prevailing perception of Japanese closed markets that ignores Japanese endeavours to open its markets. Not everyone in Europe appreciates that the import duty on cars into Japan is already zero.

We have to accept that it is not always trade barriers that make Japanese buy Japanese products or Europeans buy Japanese cars, televisions and electronic goods or Taiwanese, Hong Kong and Korean textiles. We have to be able to match Japanese quality and marketing. It is not an accident that nearly every Japanese refrigerator contains cans of Coca Cola. It has been well said that 'the consumer is not a moron; she is your wife'.

I would here emphasise that beyond common economic interests there is our sharing of long-range political and security goals that are of such extreme importance to Europe, North America, Asia and for that matter the whole free world. We must not allow these common interests to be undermined by a series of disputes about specific issues of comparatively trivial importance at least in the context of our long-term objectives.

There is undoubtedly concern in the United States and Asia about standards. There is a real worry that so called 'Euro-Standards', on whatever basis, could become a cover for blocking US, Canadian, Asian and other countries' products. As the US Deputy Secretary to the Treasury, Mr. McPherson said recently: 'Reciprocity that seeks to achieve identical commercial privileges in countries with different regulatory regimes will almost inevitably result in discrimination'. We must work together to remove these anxieties. They are indeed, anxieties that affect not only the trade between the Community and the rest of the world but also the trade between Community States. In Britain we are frequently suspicious of the sort of harmonisation that might compel us to drink 'Euro-beer' or worse still, to eat a 'Euro-sausage'. We happen to like our sausages to be mostly fried bread in a skin. After all as the Chinese proverb says: 'What is patriotism but a nostalgia for the food one ate as a child'.

I have so far considered the matter in general terms and with particular reference to trade between individual countries. It is important also to look at the position as it affects individual industries and companies in our various countries.

There are three options open to every industry and company:

1. Defensive concentrating on present traditional national and regional markets and trying to be invulnerable there. This may well be the right decision for small and medium sized companies especially those who want to remain small.

2. Continuity of established policy looking out in the usual way for new home or foreign markets or opportunities. Basically: 'Let's carry on in the way we always have'.

3. Acceptance of the need for radical change in the light not only of the changes resulting from the effects of the Single Europe Act but of the development of modern technology and global services. This may – and indeed already does – include acquisitions, mergers and joint ventures. Significantly these have taken place not just between companies in the European Community countries but also cover links of every kind with companies in America and Asia.

The European Community is essentially an area of the world where multi-national trade on a global basis in services as well as goods, does and will increasingly continue to thrive. We must make this clear to our friends in America, Asia and elsewhere.

Over the years the United States has consistantly supported our endeavours to create a more united and stronger Europe as the necessary twin pillar of the Atlantic Alliance.

I would like to conclude with a final reference to Mrs. Thatcher's speech in Bruges. Mrs. Thatcher rightly stressed the importance of our overall Alliance and the need to strengthen through WEU as well as NATO our contribution to the common defence of the free world.

We underpin our commitment to the future of Europe by recognising that we are not building a 'cash register' Europe but rather one that develops its contribution to the defence and well-being of the free world on the basis of equality.

In the light of recent political events in China and constantly evolving international situations we are fast approaching the time when we must look to Japan to make its proper contribution to the defence of the free world in the Pacific Basin, as well as to the greater liberalisation of trade. In all these matters we must see the free nations of the world working together in all fields for the good of us all. In this connection the Conservative Party in Britain in its election manifesto for the European Parliament Elections stressed its belief that, 'it is imperative to make a success of the current GATT Round as the linchpin of a more liberal world trading system'. Indeed, one of the major reasons for the creation of a Single European Market is to create an environment in which European businesses can compete internationally.

24

The Representation of UK Interests in Europe

Ann Robinson, 1989.

Dr Ann Robinson has headed the Policy Unit at the Institute of Directors. She was a member of the Economic and Social Committee and Chairman of the Industry Section.

IT is an appropriate time for me to be writing about "The Representation of UK Interests in Europe", because, after seven years of regular weekly travel to Brussels as a member of the Economic and Social Committee, I have decided that it is time for me to hand in my British Airways Executive Club Card and return my special British Airports car park pass to the British Airports Authority.

It is now seven years since I received a call from the Welsh Office asking me whether I would be willing to permit my name to go forward as a nominee for membership of the Economic and Social Committee (ESC). At that time I was teaching a large and very popular course on "The Politics of European Integration" at the University of Wales in Cardiff and I was also a very enthusiastic "Pro-European". I certainly took an active part in the promotion of the economic advantages of the European Community and its Single Market.

The opportunity to gain first-hand experience of the European political process was too good to resist and with some misgivings about the amount of travel involved I agreed. The travel immediately proved a problem. I nearly failed to arrive in Brussels for my first meeting in September 1986. Indeed, I did miss the briefings at the CBI and the Foreign Office – because on the morning of the day when I was due to travel the Severn Bridge was totally blocked and I had to drive to Heathrow via Gloucester, once I had extracted myself from the jam. This sort of mishap, I soon discovered, was par for the course. In subsequent years I suffered many long and strange journeys to and from Brussels. One good side-effect of fogs, delays, cancellations and breakdowns was that I met many very interesting fellow-travellers, with some of whom I remain in touch.

I dwell upon the travel because it is one of the things which make European Government so difficult and reduce the effectiveness of representation of interests in Brussels. It is a problem shared by other Federal states with broad territories – the USA, Canada and Australia, for example – but it is made worse in Europe because of its atomistic transport system and differences in language. The travel involved will, I believe, make things particularly difficult for the new members of the Committee of the Regions, which I will discuss later.

Although I was originally the nominee of the Welsh Office, ties between myself and Welsh interests were very tenuous. Once appointed by the Council of Ministers, I became a member of the ESC in my own right. In less formal terms, however, I was surprised that no one in Wales seemed to know what the ESC was and how it could be used to advantage. However, without an office behind me I was in no position to initiate connections which I could not service. The most active representatives at the ESC generally are closely connected to representative organizations. In part I feel that the lack of public interest in the work of the ESC is due to limited understanding of the way in which the European Community operates and a lack of appreciation that most of the laws which govern our everyday business and even personal life are affected either directly or indirectly by the law-making machine of the European Community. There is, I believe, a deep veil of ignorance about European Community matters throughout the UK. As a result the opportunities for maximizing UK influence through effective representation of UK interests are diminished. It makes no sense to speak about being "at the heart of Europe", if the blood is not being delivered to the heart for it to pump around. While other member states are not shy of using the ESC to ensure that their interests are fully taken into account, we British seem almost entirely ignorant of its existence and function.

What is the ESC and Why is it Significant?

Even I was astonished when I finally defeated the Severn Bridge and arrived at Rue Ravenstein in Brussels to discover that the ESC was not yet another small "Committee" but a sort of Parliament. It is true that the ESC has few formal powers and does not itself make legislation, but it is a real Parliament in the sense of a "place to speak" and its "Opinion" is a required element in the making of EC law. It can too easily be dismissed as a talking-shop but its voice is often sought and heard by the EC Commission in the drafting of legislation, particularly in the social field.

The ESC has its origins in the original Treaty of Rome as one of the two consultative assemblies charged with advising the Council of Ministers on the likely effects of proposed European legislation. It is worth quoting directly from the Treaty regarding its composition:

> The Committee shall consist of representatives of the various categories of economic and social activity, in particular, representatives of producers, farmers, carriers, workers, dealers, craftsmen, professional occupations and representatives of the general public.

The nature of the representation is therefore functional and expert. However, in practice the Committee has chosen to organize itself into three groups:

Group One – Employers

Group Two – Trade Unions

Group Three – Various Interests.

In practice the most powerful of these groups is Group Two, in spite of the fact that Trade Unions are hardly representative of the workers in most member states. Group One lacks the cohesive ideology which binds Group Two together, and Group Three is so diverse that it wields relatively little influence except on some details of consumer matters. The main political divisions therefore are Employers versus Trade Unions.

The Groups are the back-bone of the Committee's political organization. They determine the distribution of powerful offices such as Committee President, members of the Bureau, Section chairmanships, Rapporteurships and membership of Study Groups; and they control the use of time in Plenary debates.

The 189 members are divided between the member states according to the size of the state. Thus UK, France, Germany and Italy each have 24 members. (Germany, it should be noted, has *not* been granted additional members following reunification.) Spain has 21, Greece, The Netherlands and Portugal have 12, Denmark and Ireland have nine and Luxemburg six.

Members of the Committee are nominated by the Governments of the member states and appointed by the Council of Ministers for four-year renewable terms. Some member states let their nominees rest in Brussels for decades, others change them around from time to time. UK members generally serve for one or two terms, although one of the current delegation is now into his third term of office. Members are unpaid but receive their transport costs and extremely modest expenses. Members can appoint "Alternates", who can attend some, but not all, of the meetings in their place.

Politically, the Committee is divided into three groups. Functionally, it is divided into nine "sections". There are sections for economics and finance, industry, agriculture, environment, energy, transport and social affairs, which are responsible for processing the Committee's work namely the production of its "opinions" on proposed Community legislation for which its advice is required by the Treaty and on such matters of its own initiative as it agrees to examine.

The amount of work which 189 unpaid and part-time representatives produce is formidable. The Committee publishes some 180 "opinions" every year. These "opinions" are entirely the members' own work. I was particularly surprised, knowing that the clerks of the House of Commons and House of Lords play a large part in writing Select Committee Reports, to discover that in the ESC the member, in particular the "Rapporteur", produces the written document. The Secretariat merely runs the meetings in a formal sense.

The sections meet every month, members generally belong to three sections, and each month there is a Plenary Session which lasts for two days, requiring three days in Brussels for those members who are also on the Bureau or are Section Chairmen. This means that the minimum basic commitment is to five or six days a month in Brussels. But the most interesting part of the work is in the Study Groups which prepare the opinions for consideration in the sections. These Study Groups (of nine or 12 members generally) provide the opportunity for face-to-face interchange with Commission officials responsible for drafting legislation.

At any one time a member may be on two, three or more Study Groups and thus an active member is likely to be in Brussels two days a week. Some members opt to take office as a Section Chairman and this allows them a little more freedom of choice as to when and how often they go to meetings. Being a Chairman of a multinational committee of some 65 people, however, requires a lot of preparation and concentration – but not all of that work has to be done in Brussels itself.

The particular "plus" feature of the ESC is the expertise of its members. Some are more expert than others, it is true. But the ESC has some formidable experts in the fields of banking, insurance, automobiles, standards setting, consumer protection, agriculture, etc. This allows the ESC to shine at what it is best at – taking technical proposals and showing the possible effects which these would have in practice on industry, consumers, etc.

When the ESC takes a technical proposal, gives it into the hands of an expert Rapportcur (who in turn can appoint an expert to assist him) and an expert Study Group, it can produce opinions of great value to the Commission and the Council of Ministers. The quarterly reports sent to the ESC by the Commission reveal what proposals are taken on board. The ESC also aims to finish its work before the European Parliament completes its scrutiny, so that ESC views can be fed into the Parliament's consideration. When the ESC gets political, it sometimes helps the Commission, particularly when the Commission is acting politically, as it did over the introduction of the Social Charter. M. Delors fully understands the extent to which the ESC is a card in his hand and he has played it with great skill in the realm of the EC's "Social Dimension". On the other hand, in the long run such political statements weaken the ESC's position, for an overtly political statement on the rights of workers can always be interpreted for what it is – an expression of the fact that the unions control Group Two and that they are better whipped for voting than either Group One or Group Three. And furthermore, it is the job of the Parliament to make the political statements: it is the job of the ESC to look at practical implications.

The ESC is a significant part of the European political process in particular because it is an open and public forum –

a valuable counter-weight to the many "private" consultations with interest groups in which the Commission indulges. My last job as a member of the Committee has been to be Co-Rapporteur on the ESC "opinion" on the Report of the Sutherland Committee on implementing the Single Market. In that report we made it very clear that the process of consultation prior to legislation has to be improved and that in particular it should be more public. The ESC has a growing role to play in the consultative process, particularly now that implementation is becoming even more important than new laws. My membership coincided with a mountain of Single Market legislation and technical issues were much to the fore. In the next decade practical experience of how the single market works in practice at local level will be essential.

The Committee of the Regions

Now that the Maastricht Treaty has been ratified there will also be a "Committee of the Regions". Like the ESC it will not really be a "committee" but another parliament. Its work and procedures will be modelled largely on those of the ESC and it will share a common secretariat and facilities.

It will consist largely of members of local and regional authorities – elected representatives. If they also are in full-time employment or run their own businesses, they will find the task very difficult. It is doubtful whether anyone could combine duties as an elected councillor and as a member of the Committee of the Regions effectively, if he/she were also trying to earn a living. The logistics of combining membership of a local authority and all its various committees with membership of the Committee of the Regions and all its various sections will be formidable. The members will have to be strong and tough. However, like members of the ESC, they will be unpaid. They will, however, have the benefit of the secretarial and technical support services of their local authority behind them and thus may be able to draw on these forms of support to represent the interests of their local region.

It is difficult at this time to see how the new committee will develop. There must be some concerns about the overlap of representation between the European Parliament and the Committee of the Regions.

The Current State of European Integration

I began my work in Brussels as very much a "Pro-European". It is true that I had my own view as to what I wanted from the European Community. I saw it very much in terms of a vast open market, without borders, in which people as well as goods would have complete freedom of movement and thus greater choice and prosperity. I stated many times in countless "European" speeches that the European venture was essential to ensure the "Three Ps – Peace, Prosperity and Power". Peace because the Community would put an end to internal European wars; prosperity for the people so that they would resist the siren calls of Communism; and power so that Europeans can have a strong voice in world forums, e.g. UN and GATT.

In the mid-1980s the EC embarked on a vast programme of legislation to establish the internal market and make the terms of the Treaty of Rome a reality. Under the dynamic leadership of Jacques Delors there were real expectations of a single European Currency and Political Union by the end of this century. The circumstances were propitious. Economic growth was generally at a good level and inflation kept in check in the original six member states (except Italy) through membership of the ERM.

Today the situation is very different. Economic growth has been checked and the economies of France and Germany will shrink this year. Inflation in Germany has been encouraged by the process of reunification and hence German interest rates have been kept high to the disadvantage of other members of the ERM.

The ERM itself has virtually broken down. Unemployment is high and rising throughout the Community economies.

The European Community itself is not in a happy mood. The institutional arrangements of the Community are in a mess and there is nothing in the Maastricht Treaty which will make them work any better. There is widespread inefficiency in the way in which EC funds are spent and even evidence of corruption. In recent months, one top EC official threw himself to his death out of a window of his Brussels office and M. Crespo, the Director-General of DGV, walked out of a £120,000 job, for which he was clearly entirely unsuited. At least he had the good grace to admit that he was not up to it. Others in his position fail to recognize their incapacity and continue to draw their salary cheques. The ESC had to petition the Council of Ministers for early retirement of its Secretary-General, who, like M. Crespo, suffered from insufficient command of any except his native language.

Fortunately, in the lull before ratification of Maastricht the flood of proposed legislation reduced to a trickle, but the floodgates may open again in a year or so. As the Sutherland Committee on the Implementation of the Single Market has made clear too much proposed EC legislation is ill-researched, ill-thought out, ill-designed, poorly drafted and hastily rammed through with insufficient consultation as to its actual practical effects on the ground. The new Health and Safety rules are a case in point. There is much more which I could say on this point but I will merely conclude by stating that I am not the only person who has started out in Brussels full of enthusiasm and has retired frustrated and sceptical about the grand design. Clearly, if the venture is to succeed and not to crumble under its own inefficiencies, the EC must be reformed. It must do less and do it much better and its legislation process must become more democratic. Only then will it command the support of ordinary people.

Bringing about these reforms must be given high priority in the preparations for the review of the Maastricht process in 1996.

The Maastricht Treaty has provided a focus for popular discontent but the causes of the EC's present malaise are much deeper and more complex. No one (not even those who have read it) understands the Maastricht Treaty and can be sure of its implications. It is a colossal blank cheque. But ordinary people do understand foolish laws which prohibit the sale at a garden centre of cakes baked in a domestic kitchen. The Treaty has also suffered from terrible timing. M. Delors has always been aware of the need to hasten the "deepening" of the EC before the pressure to "widen" got too great. What made the timing so unfortunate for those who wished to establish a strong central European Union was the collapse of Communism in Eastern Europe. If we look back to the origins of the European Community in the 1950s, the fear of Communism was a potent force. So too was the French need to keep Germany under control – Germany could not be permitted to rearm and threaten European peace after three wars in the course of 70 years. The forces behind the "Three Ps" were real and strong. They are weaker now.

The same goes for European Monetary Union. There was a window of opportunity in the late 1980s, when economic growth was relatively strong and inflation under control and convergence a real prospect, but it has now closed. The economies of the EC are diverging not converging. The cost of German reunification has exposed structural weaknesses in the German economy. Once apparently impregnable as Europe's leading economy, it is now revealed as excessively expensive, and out of date. Even the great firms such as VW and Mercedes are having to struggle for survival.

The French economy and the German economy are both currently shrinking – suffering negative growth. Their

Governments have mushrooming budget deficits. Neither will be able to pay for the pensions liabilities to which they are currently committed. Only Luxemburg now meets the Maastricht criteria! With such economic weaknesses and disparities the further shock of Monetary Union could hasten industrial collapse, as it has in Eastern Germany.

France and Germany are also beginning to recognize the terrible effects of allowing the costs of employment to run out of control. Although some people in the UK still argue that we should adopt EC standards and methods of social provision, the major EC states are thinking about either reducing them or finding new ways to pay the bills. M. Balladur, the new French Prime Minister, has ordered an enquiry as to how new jobs can be created in France, whose record is dismal. The former French Socialist Government disliked part-time, temporary work, calling it "atypical", and was the driving force behind some of the dafter proposals for costly and restrictive EC-wide legislation proposed under the Commission's "Social Action Programme". With enterprise stifled in their own country they wished to level the playing-field so that we would all be equally stifled. The existence of a minimum wage in France has contributed to a very high level of unemployment. And the absurd effects of national collective bargaining for wages were clearly demonstrated by the IG Metall strike in Germany. It is amazing to realize that in some European countries private employment agencies are actually banned! That is no way to develop a mobile and flexible labour force.

So Where is "Europe" Going?

I really do not know. It is easier to say where I think it is not going. We used to hear an awful lot about the "European Train". Apparently it has a destination but we were not allowed to talk about it. No one mentions the train now. The train has no clear destination – it is more like a ghost train going round and round in circles through a tunnel full of skeletons and spectres. A few of the passengers are scared out of their wits; others (like me) are jumping out.

The European Community is not going to become a real European State – even if the Maastricht Treaty has created its legal form (and it has), because it has no popular legitimacy. The Maastricht Treaty *will* be European Law, and may come to haunt us, but it does not provide a sound and lasting constitutional foundation for the European Community's future. I have not even touched on enlargement today – but there could be new entrants in the next few years, although popular enthusiasm is no longer running assured. With the EC's institutions, budget and legal framework already, pre-Maastricht, groaning and crumbling under the burden, the most important thing now is to look forward to the Intergovernmental Conference set for 1996 and to start to ask the hitherto prohibited question "What is the destination of the Euro-Train?" What kind of European Community would be truly popular with its citizens?

I believe that we shall still want some sort of a European Community in the twenty-first century but one which is less arrogant, less Napoleonic in outlook, and much less capable of making laws which it cannot itself enforce. I have not mentioned subsidiarity because I believe it is not the solution – a sensible constitutional settlement with a division of powers is. The European Community's continued existence lies in the capacity of political leaders to respond much more to the legitimate concerns of the people who elected them – and that includes taking a clearer line on the future shape and powers of the European Community. Without that settlement all the representative Committees in the world cannot ensure political legitimacy.

25

A Question of Identity

Philip Schlesinger, 1989.

Philip Schlesinger is Professor of Film and Media Studies at the University of Stirling.

LIVING in Scotland today, on the European periphery, is bound to affect your thinking about the question of the "nation state"in Europe. North of the border, pre-existing tendencies towards separatism – and certainly autonomist demands – have been put into a new context by the re-emergence of nation states in the Baltic, by German unification, by the general disintegration of the former Soviet Union into its constituent republics and its replacement (for how long) by the Commonwealth of Independent States. Developments in Czecho-Slovakia and Yugoslavia are also being watched very closely here by the politically aware. As the United Kingdom's pre-electoral temperature rises, the national question in Scotland is becoming increasingly central. Any British government, it seems clear, will need to pay careful attention to future constitutional arrangements if it is to have a serious chance of maintaining the Union beyond another electoral term.

I do not intend to particularize for its own sake; to talk about Scotland is simply a way into the theme. If you live in a nation without a state, one endowed with a very clear national consciousness and historical distinctiveness, you are bound to rethink the dominant concept of the nation state. At moments of incipient crisis, the obviousness of the coupling between "nation" and "state" becomes relativized. And who could doubt the general and growing crisis of the nation state across Europe?

I would like to address the question by underlining the importance of questions of culture and identity. Current tendencies in Europe have put these on the political agenda in ways that can scarcely be avoided.

First, let me begin by noting that the nation state is a political configuration of modernity. But modernity is a curious condition, for, in some respects, it is characterized by flux and impermanence – what Baudelaire, in his classic formulation, identified as "the transitory, the fugitive, the contingent". It is this aspect of modernity that has been emphasized in the recent vogue for 'postmodernity' whose proponents have been apt to think that the old collectivities can no longer confer identities. We are supposed to be in a neo-tribal world where, if we don't like the company, we can opt out – nothing like the cohesive tribes of old, so it is said.

Follow this line of reasoning, and it is no surprise that one line of attack on the relative permanence of the nation state should take on a post-modern colouring. If the grand narratives are passé, and there are no compelling tales of solidarity to tell, then sure enough, the social subject can make him – or her-self afresh, in effect fashioning a new identity by choice. The structures that claim to embody identities or to confer them in relative permanence can then make few claims upon us.

Although one can sympathize with recent attempts to delineate the contemporary sense of disaggregation (especially acutely felt in some intellectual quarters, anyhow) this does not seem to reflect accurately the current situation, confusing as it doubtless is. How we think about the nation state and its relation to questions of collective identity seems to me of signal importance because, for Europeans, for around two centuries, this political form has offered an overarching normative ideal of collective identification.

In Europe, as is well known, the nation state has come into existence over a lengthy time-span and by quite distinct development paths. Looked at from this point of view, the European Community's construction has something of the character of the administrative-bureaucratic mode of state formation, rather than the quest by an ethnic group to create a state for itself. A set of nation states is in the process of trying to fashion an over-arching political structure – in effect, to create a state. Political union, a common economic space, a common defence identity, all point to the key appurtenances of statehood.

Post-Maastricht, the euphemism "ever closer union" may, for some British politicians, be a phrase more acceptable than "federalism". But, however one finesses it, the *ultima ratio* of the current integration process surely eventually points to a central source of political legitimacy in the EC, disposing of a monopoly of the means of violence. This is part of our modern understanding of the prerequisites for statehood. And the rather faltering steps taken towards a so-called European defence identity proclaim such a recognition, as does the oft uttered trope that Europe should now recognize its superpower status in the world.

As yet, the ultimate boundaries of the emergent Eurostate remain undefined – the eventual accession of the EFTA countries, and of other states in the former Communist bloc, will ensure that this remains unresolved for the foreseeable future. One question to be posed in relation to such future enlargement is whether we can plausibly conceive of talking of an eventual European *nation* state. To be a "European" is different from being a member of a "European nation". The latter, much more acutely than the former, raises an unavoidable cultural question about what collective political identities might be possible.

To get the measure of the problem it is worth considering what is involved in talking about collective identities – that is, the means whereby collectivities construct and reconstruct a sense of themselves by reference to the signs provided by cultures.

Briefly, my position is this. First, the making of identities is an active process that involves inclusion and exclusion. To be 'us', we need those who are "not us". Second, the imaginary process of creating traditions and of activating collective memories extends through time. The dark side of memory is amnesia; to shed light is also to throw shadows. Third, collective identities have a spatial referent, although this need not always conform to a model of territorial concentration and juridico-political integrity. In Europe, however, the primordial attachment does seem to be to a land or territory.

Currently, the supranationalist quest in Europe is compelling us to rethink the nature of the nation state – a political, economic and cultural entity that is identity-conferring. European statehood, whatever concessions are made to 'subsidiarity', will change the scope of contemporary conceptions of citizenship: the rights and duties of citizens will be redefined and the scope of allegiances shifted. Classical conceptions of political sovereignty, where the political actor is the nation state in a world made up of nation states, will have to be revised – and in some quarters this is perceived as inducing a crisis of political identity. It is crucial to the eventual success of European political unity that the democratic deficit be overcome and that crises of representation be avoided. An especial challenge arises in respect of centre-periphery relations and the devising of modes of representation that take account of the real heterogeneity of Europe. Amongst other things, this will involve recognizing the potential and actual internal diversity of the nation state within any larger supranational configuration.

Euro-integrationism, then, is one quest for ultimate statehood, with what results one can only presently conjecture. Within the boundaries of the EC, there are stirrings of regionalisms with a nationalist potentiality; in Scotland, increasingly in Wales, in Catalonia and the Basque Country. There are hopes in these places, for instance, that the road to Brussels can bypass London and Madrid. In that sense, processes of integration at the level of the EC could be said to be producing disintegration at the level of the nation state, by way of the variable impact of the uneven development of capitalism. It is not clear how these pressures, in turn, will transform the present character of the nation state. Whether these so-called neo-nationalisms turn into a separate quest for nation statehood, fuelled by a sense of politico-cultural difference, remains to be seen. There is currently a vested interest on the part of central state governments and regionalists alike to fudge the issue. But it is reasonable to ask whether a Europe of the Regions is not ultimately in contradiction with a Europe of the Nation States.

Nobody yet knows whether the EC will eventually constitute an umbrella framework for all European states. We hear much less about the Common European Home than a couple of years ago. Against the proposed deepening of European Community links it is suggested that they be extended to take in nations from Central and Eastern Europe. But to what extent? When there was still a Soviet Union, some proposed its exclusion on grounds of size, others on cultural grounds. Which of the new republics will now pass the qualifying test and why? One must ask, because Central Europe's designation by Milan Kundera some years ago as a kidnapped part of the West has its echoes in contemporary strategic thinking. The formula has been recodified by asking where the writ of Roman

Catholicism stops and where Orthodoxy begins. Thus religious designation does the work of politico-cultural distinction. In related vein, the problematic position of Turkey as a Muslim country periodically resurfaces. This links into a much broader question of the position of Islamic minorities in Europe.

Currently, despite the drive towards European unity, counter-tendencies are only too much in evidence. The crisis of nationalities and state structures in ex-Yugoslavia and in the ex-Soviet Union is provoking a diffuse sense of difference in Europe. The rebirth of history in the shape of this ethnonational reawakening is leading to new configurations between nations and states, but in ways that are not yet clearcut. The unresolved boundary questions between other states that cut through national groups – Hungary and Romania, for instance – or between component nationalities – as in Czecho-Slovakia – raise many questions about the future of pacific conflict resolution in Europe. I would simply reflect that two nation states – the UK and Irish Republic – have not been able to resolve the nationalist insurgency in Northern Ireland. EC membership on the part of each would appear to be little more than an irrelevance. And here we are not talking about a border dispute that represents a potential *casus belli*. Although containable, such conflicts are costly, with long-term negative consequences for a democratic order, as the British know only too well.

If we shift the focus again to the EC, fears of an incipient "Fortress Europe" appear to be borne out by current developments. Specifically, the extreme and often violent racist reaction to migration currently so much in evidence in Belgium, France, Italy and Germany makes one pose some further questions about how we might arrive at a transcendent "Europeanism" that must needs embrace the vast diversity and complexity of this continent. In Britain, this level of reaction has not yet been reached, but links between the Continental extreme right and its British counterparts are actively being forged and the imminent tightening up of the right to asylum is a good index of the xenophobia that lies just beneath the surface.

Current racism and anti-Semitism in Western Europe are, to some extent, the counterparts of the resurgent ethno-nationalism in the old East. Characteristically, much of this new wave takes refuge in an essentialist conception of the nation: if your race or culture or religion do not fit the parameters, then you cannot belong. How can this neo-nationalism – with its strong Nazi overtones – be accommodated by an expansive conception of Europeanness? It marks a rejection of pluriculturalism and if this becomes a respectable political project – which it shows every sign of doing – the prospects for building civic national identities will become seriously weakened. Whatever the distinctive motivations and causes, the demand for pure identities within the major Western nation states would seem to be for a simpler world, purged of ambiguity. Europe's current demographic panic, in which nervous eyes are cast to the southern Mediterranean and towards the east of the German frontiers, are also part of this tendency.

My own perspective on the tensions that presently beset the nation state in Europe compels me to note the paradoxical character of today's developments. On the one hand, the difficult search for a transcendent unity which must recognize component differences throws the nation state into question from above. On the other hand, the ethno-nationalist awakenings in the former Communist bloc, and also within Western Europe – whether neo-nationalist or reactionary racist – tend to reaffirm the principle of the nation state as a locus of identity.

Thus, Europe is simultaneously undergoing processes of centralization and of fragmentation. These processes pass through the nation state and the impact is strongly focused on questions of collective identity. The present confusion that we face has thrown established modes of political analysis, substantially shaped by the Cold War, into disarray, particularly with respect to the former East, where how to characterize the emergent transitional regimes remains a question on the agenda.

It will be obvious that I think that sensitivity to complexity and tolerance of diversity will be indispensable to all Europeans. This sounds pious indeed and it is quite justifiable to place a question mark over the pluralistic conception of the political and social order that underpins it, as such a conception does not command universal assent and looks as though it is coming under increasing strain.

26

Britain's European Heritage

Norman Stone, 1990.

Norman Stone is Professor of Modern History at Oxford University.

THE most famous line in that famous film, *The Third Man*, is Orson Welles's comparison of Italy and Switzerland. Italy, with endless crime and mayhem, produced the Renaissance; Switzerland, after five hundred years of peace and brotherly love, produced – the cuckoo clock. This is a good crack, and probably true in spirit: small, prosperous, well-organised and neutral countries are not, nowadays, culturally very interesting, and it is worth saying that the ramshackle, oppressive and heavily polluted countries of eastern and central Europe have produced, in the last generation, more interesting novelists and film-makers than several countries to the West.

But, historically speaking, Orson Welles's famous crack has it wrong. Switzerland's civilization is a long, long way from being either sterile or peaceful. Since the days of William Tell or Charles the Bold of Burgundy's efforts to crush them in the later fifteenth century, the Swiss fought. They had a fierce, provincial pride, of the kind that easily turned towards Protestantism, and in particular Calvinism. Geneva, in Calvin's time, was a theocratic police-state; it also made a good bit of money, since trade from Lyons to Venice passed through it. 'Companions of the Oath' – Eidgenossen – were the Swiss equivalent of the Scottish Covenanters in Charles II's time, and their name, corrupted into French, became Huguenot. Calvinism, banking, education, went together in the seventeenth centuries and later in Switzerland, France, the Netherlands, Scotland and England: la Haute Société Protestante was an international phenomenon. Switzerland was partly Catholic, but for long the Calvinists were predominant. There were civil wars in Switzerland up to the mid-nineteenth century, and there were general strikes in the twentieth. There is no sense in which Swiss history can be described as dull.

Nor was the country culturally sterile in the way that Welles supposed: quite the contrary. As happened with Scotland – also poor and mountainous; also divided in religion, with a ferocious Calvinism prominent early on; also with a startlingly different version of the language – ferocious Calvinism, once civilized, produced an interesting civilization in the eighteenth and nineteenth centuries. Gibbon spent much time there, and not by accident; Benjamin Constant, Voltaire, Rousseau (and others, on the German side, though we know them less well) were in some degree or another associated with Switzerland. As with the Scots the technical side flourished – banks, obviously enough, but also medicine (many of the doctors and biologists ending up in France) and inventions. It is in that context that we should see the cuckoo-clock. It was not a kitsch-tourist affair at all, but one outcome of a poor, mountain-peasant world in which humble people, surrounded for long months by snow, worked out the practicalities of time-keeping. David Landes wrote a wonderful book on the history of time-keeping, and the Swiss of course come top: even humble peasants could be highly inventive in precision-tools and in the division of labour, with use of credit and of commercial middle-men to arrange the retailing of these cheap, but sturdy and efficient time-pieces. Thoughts about such things led several Swiss to think about political economy, as they led several Scots: the Say of Say's Law versus Adam Smith for instance.

There was a time when England's Industrial Revolution held the centre of our historical stage. In the 1960s, there was a kind of Lord Snow version of the Whig Interpretation. Just as great historians – Macaulay above all – presented the country's history as a long development of Liberty, culminating in the Whigs' overthrow of Reaction and subsequently therefore able to produce Democracy via nineteenth-century Reform, so there was an up-dated economic counterpart later on. Technologists fought against backwardness, whether in agriculture or industry; population grew; women were – relatively – decently treated; there was less inequality and so there was Demand: a mass-market, which could be used as a parable, in a way, for the 1960s. An extremely good essay, on these lines, was written by Neil McKendrick – who taught me in my extreme youth, to my very great profit, because I learned economic history and much else from him – in a Festschrift for Sir J.H. Plumb, the main neo-Snowite in these matters. But can England – I use the name consciously, being a Scotsman – really be as complacent, post-Wilson, about these matters as we used to be?

For the fact of the matter is that the Industrial Revolution did not really happen. It was also not unique, and it was also not English. Scratch the surface of the thing, and you find that no-one was conscious of it at the time – the very name came about much later, via something that the French in the 1830s knew as 'the system of machines' in the 1870s. The inventions were of course important, but in the eighteenth century they were mainly Scottish: the roads, canals, the machinery. Not entirely, but still. In those days, continentals did not bother with Oxford or Cambridge, institutions of a mediaeval character that flourished mainly because their bursars were quite good at parasiting upon money made by other people, to the North. Constant and the secularized Protestant international- they included, in a different way, and later, Tocqueville – made for Edinburgh, where the Scottish Enlightenment was pro- fessed.

The Industrial Revolution occurred in the nineteenth century, especially with the railways and the urbanization that they permitted. The eighteenth century laid the groundwork for this: attitudes of mind, legal prescriptions, scientific princi- ples. The Scottish Enlightenment had the most powerful role in all of this, and the products of that period, in the next gen- eration, ran England: directly or indirectly, they include Brougham, Gladstone, Mill, Macaulay, and whole hosts of entrepreneurs and technologists. Mirabeau remarked of Prussia that she was 'hatched from a cannon-ball'. The same was true of the Lowland Scots in the eighteenth century, though in a different, educational sense. Their marriage with England was endlessly fertile, because the drive of Calvinism went together with a political structure that could civilize it.

England herself, in this perspective, is a unique creation because she was the only one of the European *anciens regimes* to survive. Here was a Church that held the country together, as sectarians could not do (witness the disintegration of Germany, or even the Netherlands). But it was not a truly oppressive Church, in the manner of Counter-Reformation Catholicism, and though it might Test-Act, it did not torture. Here, too, was a monarchy and a court that kept the country together without tyrannizing: for *lettre de cachet* read *habeas corpus* throughout. Burke remarked of the English constitu- tion: 'so we proceed from light to light. We compromise, we reconcile, we balance'. And so we did, often without recourse to formal law. Serfdom dwindled and died in England early on. No-one really defended it; it just collapsed, and its collapse never appeared on the Statute Books. Not until 1925, when F.E. Smith was tidying up the Law, was 'copyhold' abolished, the nearest equivalent to serfdom, and I often want to put that in as an examination question, with 'Discuss' attached. The marriage of England and Scotland was such a powerful affair that it eventually took over a quarter of the world's land surface. In modern times, the British Isles were seen by their own educated inhabitants as unique, because of this. At Oxford, where I profess European history, English history still takes up an enormous part of the curriculum and everything else is squeezed up into 'General History' (apart from the various special subjects). European History is something apart from English History. Now, with the Empire gone, and with neither England nor Scotland what they were, we should re-think these things. For the fact is that British civilization, though outstanding in what it produced, is very much a part of European civilization in general. The main strands in it are European, but with only a modified version of the conflicts that occurred between such strands elsewhere in the continent. Calvinism in education, without the Witches-of-Salem connotations, is one; pre-Counter-Reformation Catholicism – which is what Anglicanism is without the doziness – the other. Why these two things worked in the British Isles is a good question. And now, given the collapse of the religious worldview, where it all leaves us is another one. The central problem, of a northern Protestant work-ethic as opposed to the skills in politics of a Mediterranean-Catholic world, is clearly still with us: in the Third Republic, they used to say 'C'est le Nord qui travaille et le Midi qui gouverne'. In the new Europe, it is something to beware of, because it risks leaving this country with a political cuckoo-clock. When I hear that 'Europe', as constituted, costs us well over four thousand million pounds per annum I wonder if someone, somewhere, is not taking us for a ride.

27

European Family of Nations

Margaret Thatcher, 1989.

Lady Thatcher was British Prime Minister from 1979-1990.

MY recent speech in Belgium gave me the opportunity to return to Bruges in very different circumstances from my previous visit shortly after the Zeebrugge ferry disaster, when Belgian courage and the devotion of their doctors and nurses had saved so many British lives. It was a great pleasure to speak at the College of Europe, under the distinguished leadership of its Rector, Professor Lukaszewski, which plays a vital and increasingly important part in the life of the European Community. I was especially pleased to deliver my address in that magnificent hall. What better place could be found to speak on Europe's future than in a building which so gloriously recalls the greatness that Europe had already achieved over 600 years ago? The city of Bruges has many other historical associations for us in Britain; Geoffrey Chaucer was a frequent visitor and the first book to be printed in the English language was produced there by William Caxton.

I was invited to speak on the subject of Britain and Europe and I said that perhaps they should be congratulated on their courage; for if they believed some of the things said and written about my views on Europe, it must have seemed rather like inviting Genghis Khan to speak on the virtues of peaceful co-existence! I started by disposing of some myths about Britain, and its relationship with Europe, and to do that I had to say something about the identity of Europe itself. Europe is not the creation of the Treaty of Rome, nor is the European idea the property of any group or institution. We British are as much heirs to the legacy of European culture as any other nation. Our links to the rest of Europe, the continent of Europe, have been the dominant factor in our history. For three hundred years we were part of the Roman Empire and our maps still trace the straight lines of the roads the Romans built. Our ancestors – Celts, Saxons and Danes – came from the continent. Our nation was – in that favourite Community word – 'restructured' under Norman and Angevin rule in the eleventh and twelfth centuries. This year we celebrate the three hundredth anniversary of the Glorious Revolution in which the British crown passed to Prince William of Orange and Queen Mary. Visit the great Churches and Cathedrals of Britain, read our literature and listen to our language: all bear witness to the cultural riches which we have drawn from Europe – and other Europeans from us. We are rightly proud of the way in which, since Magna Carta in 1215, we have pioneered and developed representative institutions to stand as bastions of freedom. And proud too of the way in which for centuries Britain was a home for people from the rest of Europe who sought sanctuary from tyranny. But we know that without the European legacy of political ideas we could not have achieved as much as we did. From classical and medieval thought we have borrowed that concept of the rule of law which marks out a civilised society from barbarism. And on that idea of Christendom – for long synonymous with Europe – with its recognition of the unique and spiritual nature of the individual, we still base our belief in personal liberty and other human rights.

Too often the history of Europe is described as a series of interminable wars and quarrels. Yet from our perspective today surely what strikes us most is our common experience. For instance, the story of how Europeans explored and colonised and – yes, without apology – civilised much of the world is an extraordinary tale of talent, skill and courage. We British have in a special way contributed to Europe. Over the centuries we have fought to prevent Europe from falling under the dominance of a single power. We have fought and we have died for her freedom. Only a few miles from Bruges lie the bodies of 120,000 British soldiers who died in the First World War. Had it not been for their willingness to fight and to die, Europe would have been united long before now – but not in liberty, not in justice. It was British support to resistance movements throughout the last War that helped to keep alive the flame of liberty in so many countries until the day of liberation. The day after my speech, King Baudouin attended a service in Brussels to commemorate the many brave Belgians who gave their lives in service with the Royal Air Force – a sacrifice which we shall never forget. It was from our island fortress that the liberation of Europe itself was mounted. And still today we stand together. Nearly 70,000 British servicemen are stationed on the mainland of Europe. All these things alone are proof of our commitment to Europe's future. The European Community is *one* manifestation of that European identity, but it is not the only one. We must never forget that East of the Iron Curtain peoples who once enjoyed a full share of European culture, freedom and identity have been cut off from their roots. We shall always look on Warsaw, Prague and Budapest as great European cities. Nor should we forget that European values have helped to make the United States of America into the valiant defender of freedom which she has become.

This is no arid chronicle of obscure facts from the dust-filled libraries of history. It is the record of nearly two thousand years of British involvement in Europe, co-operation *with*

Europe and contribution *to* Europe, a contribution which today is as valid and as strong as ever. Yes, we have looked also to wider horizons – as have others – and thank goodness for that, because Europe never would have prospered and never will prosper as a narrow-minded, inward-looking club. The European Community belongs to *all* its members. It must reflect the traditions and aspirations of *all* of them in full measure. Britain does not dream of some cosy, isolated existence on the fringes of the European Community. Our destiny is in Europe, as part of the Community. That is not to say that our future lies *only* in Europe – but nor does that of France or Spain or indeed any other member. The Community is not an end in itself, nor is it an institutional device to be constantly modified according to the dictates of some abstract intellectual concept. Nor must it be ossified by endless regulation. The European Community is the practical means by which Europe can ensure the future prosperity and security of its people in a world in which there are many other powerful nations and groups of nations. We Europeans cannot afford to waste our energies on internal disputes or arcane institutional debates. They are no substitutes for effective action. Europe has to be ready both to contribute in full measure to its own security and to compete commercially and industrially, in a world in which success goes to the countries which encourage individual initiative and enterprise, rather than to those which attempt to diminish them.

In my speech I set out some guiding principles for the future which I believe will ensure that Europe *does* succeed, not just in economic and defence terms but also in the quality of life and the influence of its peoples.

My first guiding principle is this: willing and active co-operation between independent sovereign states is the best way to build a successful European Community. To try to suppress nationhood and concentrate power at the centre of a European conglomerate would be highly damaging and would jeopardize the objectives we seek to achieve. Europe will be stronger precisely because it has France as France, Spain as Spain, Britain as Britain, each with its own customs, traditions and identity. It would be folly to try to fit them into some sort of identikit European personality. Some of the founding fathers of the Community thought that the United States of America might be its model, but the whole history of America is quite different from Europe. People went there to get away from the intolerance and constraints of life in Europe. They sought liberty and opportunity; and their strong sense of purpose has, over two centuries, helped create a new unity and pride in being American – just as our pride lies in being British or Belgian or Dutch or German. I am the first to say that on many great issues the countries of Europe should try to speak with a single voice. I want to see us work more closely on the things we can do better together than alone. Europe is stronger when we do so, whether it be in trade, in defence, or in our relations with the rest of the world. But working more closely together does *not* require power to be centralised in Brussels or decisions to be taken by an appointed bureaucracy. Indeed, it is ironic that just when those countries such as the Soviet Union, which have tried to run everything from the centre, are learning that success depends on dispersing power and decisions *away* from the centre, some in the Community seem to want to move in the opposite direction. We have not successfully rolled back the frontiers of the state in Britain, only to see them reimposed at a European level, with a European super-state exercising a new dominance from Brussels. Certainly we want to see Europe more united and with a greater sense of common purpose, but it must be in a way which preserves the different traditions, parliamentary powers and sense of national pride in one's own country, for these have been the source of Europe's vitality through the centuries.

My second guiding principle is this. Community policies must tackle present problems in a *practical* way, however difficult that may be. If we cannot reform those Community policies which are patently wrong or ineffective and which are rightly causing public disquiet, then we shall not get the public's support for the Community's future development. That is why the achievements of the European Council in Brussels last February are so important. It wasn't right that half the total Community Budget was being spent on storing and disposing of surplus food. Now those stocks are being sharply reduced. It was absolutely right to decide that agriculture's share of the budget should be cut in order to free resources for other policies, such as helping the less well off regions and training for jobs. It was right too to introduce tighter budgetary discipline to enforce these decisions and to bring total EC spending under better control. Those who complained that the Community was spending so much time on financial detail missed the point. You cannot build on unsound foundations, financial or otherwise and it was the fundamental reforms agreed last winter which paved the way for the remarkable progress which we have since made on the Single Market, but we cannot rest on what we have achieved to date. For example, the task of reforming the Common Agricultural Policy is far from complete. Certainly, Europe needs a stable and efficient farming industry, but the CAP has become unwieldy, inefficient and grossly expensive. Production of unwanted surpluses safeguards neither the income nor the future of farmers themselves. We must *continue* to pursue policies which relate supply more closely to market require-ments, and which will reduce overproduction and limit costs. Of course, we must protect the villages and rural areas which are such an important part of our national life – but not by the instrument of agricultural prices. Tackling these problems requires political courage. The Community will only damage itself in the eyes of its own people and the outside world if that courage is lacking.

My third guiding principle is the need for Community policies which encourage enterprise. If Europe is to flourish and create the jobs of the future, enterprise is the key. The basic framework is there: the Treaty of Rome itself was intended as a Charter for Economic Liberty. But that is not how it has always been read, still less applied. The lesson of the economic history of Europe in the 70s and 80s is that central planning and detailed control *don't* work, and that personal endeavour and initiative *do*; that a State-controlled economy is a recipe for low growth, and that free enterprise within a framework of law brings better results. The aim of a Europe open to enterprise is the moving force behind the creation of the Single European Market by 1992. By getting rid of barriers, by making it possible for companies to operate on a Europe-wide scale, we can best compete with the United States, Japan and the other new economic powers emerging in Asia and elsewhere – and that means action to free markets, action to *widen* choice, action to reduce government intervention. Our aim should not be more and more detailed regulation from the centre: it should be to deregulate and to remove the constraints on trade. Britain has been in the lead in opening its markets to others. The City of London has long welcomed financial institutions from all over the world, which is why it is the biggest and most successful financial centre in Europe. We have opened our market for telecommunications equipment, introduced competition into the market for services and even into the network itself – steps which others in Europe are only now beginning to face. In air transport, we have taken the lead in liberalisation and seen the benefits in cheaper fares and wider choice. Our coastal shipping trade is open to the merchant navies of Europe. I wish I could say the same of many other Community members. Regarding monetary matters, let me say this. The key issue is *not* whether there should be a European Central Bank. The immediate and practical requirements are to implement the Community's commitment to free movement of capital – in Britain we have it – and to the abolition throughout the Community of the exchange controls – in Britain we abolished them in *1979* – to establish a genuinely free market in financial services, in banking, insurance, investment – to make greater use of the ecu – Britain is this autumn issuing ecu-denominated Treasury bills, and hopes to see other Community governments increasingly do the same.

These are the *real* requirements, because they are what Community business and industry need if they are to compete effectively in the wider world. And they are what the European consumer wants, for they will widen his choice and lower his costs. It is to such basic practical steps that the Community's attention should be devoted. When those have been achieved, and sustained over a period of time, we shall be in a better position to judge the next moves.

It is the same with the frontiers between our countries. Of course we must make it easier for goods to pass through frontiers. Of course we must make it easier for our people to travel throughout the Community. But it is a matter of plain commonsense that we cannot totally abolish frontier controls if we are also to protect our citizens from crime and stop the movement of drugs, of terrorists, and of illegal immigrants that was underlined graphically only weeks ago, when one brave German customs officer, doing his duty on the frontier between Holland and Germany, struck a major blow against the terrorists of the IRA.

Before leaving the subject of the Single Market, I would add that we certainly do not need new regulations which raise the cost of employment and make Europe's labour market less flexible and less competitive with overseas suppliers. If we are to have a European Company Statute, it should contain the minimum regulations, and certainly we in Britain would fight attempts to introduce collectivism and corporatism at the European level – although what people wish to do in their own countries is a matter for them.

My fourth guiding principle is that Europe should not be protectionist. The expansion of the world economy requires us to continue the process of removing barriers to trade, and to do so in the multilateral negotiations in the GATT. It would be a betrayal if, while breaking down constraints on trade within Europe, the Community were to erect greater external protection. We must ensure that our approach to world trade is consistent with the liberalisation we preach at home. We have a responsibility to give a lead on this, a responsibility which is particularly directed towards the less developed countries. They need not only aid, more than anything they need improved trading opportunities if they are to gain the dignity of growing economic strength and independence.

My last guiding principle concerns the most fundamental issue, the European countries' role in defence. Europe must continue to maintain a sure defence through NATO. There can be no question of relaxing our efforts even though it means taking difficult decisions and meeting heavy costs. It is to NATO that we owe the peace that has been maintained over 40 years. The fact is things are going our way: the democratic model of a free enterprise society has proved itself superior; freedom is on the offensive, a peaceful offensive, the world over for the first time in my life-time. We must strive to maintain the United States' commitment to Europe's defence. That means recognising the burden on their resources of the world role they undertake, and their point that their allies should play a full part in the defence of freedom, particularly as Europe grows wealthier. Increasingly they will look to Europe to play a part in out-of-area defence, as we have recently done in the Gulf. NATO and the WEU have long recognised where the problems with Europe's defences lie, and have pointed out the solutions. The time has come when we must give substance to our declarations about a strong defence effort with better value for money. It is not an institutional problem, nor a problem of drafting, but something at once simpler and more profound: it is a question of political will and political courage, of convincing people in all our countries that we cannot rely for ever on others for our defence, but that each member of the Alliance must shoulder a fair share of the burden. We must keep up public support for nuclear deterrence, remembering that obsolete weapons do not deter, hence the need for modernisation. We must meet the requirements for effective conventional defence in Europe against Soviet forces which are constantly being modernised. We should develop the WEU, not as an alternative to NATO, but as a means of strengthening Europe's contribution to the common defence of the West. Above all at a time of change and uncertainty in the Soviet Union and Eastern Europe, we must preserve Europe's unity and resolve, so that whatever may happen our defence is sure. At the same time, we must negotiate on arms control and keep the door wide open to co-operation on all the other issues covered by the Helsinki Accords, but let us never forget that our way of life, our vision, and all that we hope to achieve is secured not by the rightness of our cause but by the strength of our defence. On this we must never falter, never fall.

I believe it is not enough just to talk in general terms about a European vision or ideal. If we believe in it we must chart the way ahead and identify the next steps. That's what I have always tried to do. This approach does not require new documents: they are all there, the North Atlantic Treaty, the Revised Brussels Treaty, and the Treaty of Rome, texts written by far-sighted men, a remarkable Belgian – Paul Henri Spaak – among them. However far we may want to go, the truth is that we can only get there one step at a time. What we need now is to take decisions on the next steps forward rather than let ourselves be distracted by Utopian goals. Utopia never comes, because we know we should not like it if it did.

Let Europe be a family of nations, understanding each other better, appreciating each other more, doing more together but relishing our national identity no less than our common European endeavour. Let us have a Europe which plays its full part in the wider world, which looks outward not inward, and which preserves that Atlantic Community – that Europe on both sides of the Atlantic – which is our noblest inheritance and our greatest strength.

28

The Real Questions for Europe

Christopher Tugendhat, 1989.

Lord Tugendhat was Vice President of the European Commission and Chairman of the Royal Institute of International Affairs.

THE British Prime Minister's now celebrated speech at Bruges on the future of Europe has put the question of how the European Community should develop very much onto the political agenda. With elections to the European Parliament due in 1989 the debate is likely to gather momentum over the next few months. Attention has so far been devoted primarily to the age old question of whether we should think in terms of a United States of Europe or a Europe des Parties, to use General de Gaulle's words. There are, however, other more important aspects that should also be addressed.

I say more important because the die has long since been cast so far as the choice between a United States of Europe and a *Europe des Parties* is concerned. Whatever policies or co-operative ventures the Community undertakes, one thing is certain. It will develop on the basis of the nation states rather than supranational institutions. General de Gaulle himself made certain of that back in the 1960s. The subsequent enlargements that have doubled the membership from six to twelve have completed the task.

There was never really any doubt about the outcome. In the immediate post war period the concepts of nationality and the nation state had in many parts of Europe, though for obvious reasons not in Britain, been widely discredited. The ideal of universal reconciliation and the aspiration to build a brave new world led naturally to federalism. It was a noble impulse and without its moral force the Community might not have been founded and would certainly not have developed as quickly as it did. But once the memories of the war began to diminish and economies to recover it was always likely that it would fade.

For some 400 years Europeans have defined themselves primarily in terms of nationality and the nation state. Some peoples adopted the concept relatively early, others later, but since the sixteenth century nationalism has been the foundation on which the great majority of Europeans have wished to build their political structures. As a result it is only the nation state that can command loyalty and obedience, and in the twentieth century only governments elected on the basis of a national and universal suffrage that are regarded as legitimate.

Against this background it would run counter not just to the grain of history but also to social realities to attempt to build a European superstate designed to replace the individual nation states. The federal dream is still alive and because of the part it played in bringing Europeans together after the war and launching the Community it is held in respect by many who do not, in practice, subscribe to it. For that reason attacks upon it are widely and deeply resented. They are also likely to lead many who do not, in practice, live by the ideal vigorously to restate it while hitting back at the assailant. Nevertheless, there is no government nor any significant body of opinion in any member state that in real terms plans on anything other than a *Europe des Parties*.

In Britain this point is widely misunderstood in part for reasons of political terminology. We talk of powers being handed over to Brussels or policies being run from Brussels as if Brussels is some sort of self-contained entity separate and apart from Britain to which sovereignty is given or withheld. The reality is quite different. When a policy is carried out at Community level, governments do not hand over sovereignty, they share it. That is to say they agree in the Council of Ministers that something should be done on a Community basis and how it should be done. The Commission puts forward proposals that the Council may or may not accept and carries out the subsequent decision in accordance with the Council's wishes and under its supervision.

There can be no question of a group of states forcing one or a number into line. That would be quite contrary both to the principle of free association that underlies the Community and of the ultimate supremacy of governments elected by universal suffrage on a national basis. When a Community objective is set, or new policy or venture undertaken, it must have the explicit support of all participants. That is, for instance, the case with the Single European Market even though it is an objective restated rather than an entirely new one. However, once governments have committed themselves to achieving something, especially when they have agreed a target date as well, it is perfectly reasonable for them to accept that differences between them on matters of detail should be resolved by majority voting.

If a government feels it cannot go along with the new objective or enterprise in the first place, it must accept that the corollary of opting out is that others may proceed without it. In effect, that is what has happened in relation to Britain and the exchange rate mechanism of the European Monetary System. In making this judgement the government concerned must consider its own interests not only in connection with the point at issue but also in terms of the implications of being left out, especially if it feels it may subsequently wish to join after the rules have been written.

Thus the real question at the present time is not whether there will be a European superstate. It is a quite different but also very important one of what sort of policies and how many should be conducted on a European basis and what should be left to the individual Member States. Just as there are those in domestic politics who would like to see a powerful state actively involved in all aspects of economic affairs and influencing wide areas of people's lives, so there are those who believe that Europe should be organised in a similar fashion. The real argument at the present time is, as has long been the case in the domestic politics of many countries, between the advocates of extensive government intervention in the economy and far reaching industrial and technological support on the one hand and their opponents on the other.

In this debate neither side can claim to be more or less European than the other any more than in 1980, Jimmy Carter who favoured big government and more power to Washington at the expense of the states, could claim to be more American than Ronald Reagan who preached the reverse. Nor should the President of the European Commission, or even the Commission itself, be regarded as an arbiter of orthodoxy either way. The Commission has a duty to which, in my experience, it invariably seeks to adhere, to pursue the general interest rather than that of any of its parts. But like any established body it has its own theories and objectives, some of which remain constant, and others of which change with the personalities and politics of its members.

All member states have committed themselves to the promotion of European unity by accepting the Treaty of Rome in the first place and subsequently by signing the Single European Act. The Commission is equally bound both to encourage them down this road and to point the way forward. These basic points like any other treaty, or constitutional obligation, should not be forgotten, and any government that gives the impression of not taking them seriously lays itself open to attack from its partners. Their own motives may be self serving or even hypocritical. They may, in reality, be pleased to have an excuse to shy away from issues they do not want to confront. Nonetheless, governments that wish to influence the actions of others and to play a leading role in the future development of Europe must be extremely careful not to put themselves in a position where others can credibly question their good faith and cast them as scapegoats in the event of an impasse.

The style of British politics is adversarial with two great armies drawn up against each other and issues defined in clear cut terms. Faced with a choice the electorate must plump for one or the other. Those who have tried to break the mould by interposing a third force and making the search for common ground the principal objective have, to date at any rate, found themselves broken by the system. Diplomacy has, of course, traditionally been conducted according to different rules. But relations between the Member States of the Community have become so intimate and cover such a wide range of previously purely domestic matters – agriculture, industry, the environment, competition law, etc – that they are treated in all countries more as an extension of domestic politics than as a branch of diplomacy.

This puts those brought up in the British political tradition at something of a disadvantage since in a system in which all the participants are sovereign independent states there can be no question of a simple choice between two rival armies and two rival theories. Those who wish to lead must do so by forming alliances and coalitions and by being prepared to compromise on some objectives in order to achieve others. The style and skills required come more easily to politicians brought up in countries with multi-party politics where dealing with other parliamentary groups is as important if not more so than winning the support of the electorate.

In these circumstances, both the advocates of big government on a Europe-wide scale and their opponents need to examine their positions carefully.

Those who support the proposition must bear in mind that when twelve countries are involved, agreement is inevitably difficult to reach and Member States are more likely to arrive at common positions if faced with a limited number of decisions. This does not mean that anyone should be modest in their aspirations; what it does require is a recognition that if the Community is faced with too many decisions at any one time it will be incapacitated by indigestion. The best test of a proposal, apart from whether it responds to a real need is whether, if implemented, it would in practice unite or disunite the Member States. Unity should be regarded not simply as an aim but also as a test. The establishment of a Single European Market meets this criterion since it would not only hope to integrate the economies of the Member States but would also enable their citizens to travel, settle and work wheresoever they pleased. By contrast, an attempt to harmonise the constitutions of the Member States, to take an extreme example, would set people at each other's throats.

For their part the decentralisers and advocates of states' rights must recognise that in the Community if you order the meat dish you have to eat the potatoes as well. Thus, de Gaulle could not have had the Common Agricultural Policy, which he wanted, without the elimination of tariffs on manufactured goods, which the Germans insisted upon and which, in any case, created a complementary and self-reinforcing package. Similar considerations apply now to the Single European Market which the British Government wants, and to closer economic and monetary co-operation. Not only is there a political imperative but the former is, in any case, unsustainable without the latter.

Moreover, it is impossible to run a Single European Market in isolation from other matters. If goods on sale in one country are to be sold in others there have to be mutually acceptable standards between the states concerned. If financial institutions are to offer their services across frontiers the prudential standards governing their affairs must also be mutually acceptable as well as comprehensible to all. If citizens are to be free to work wherever they wish, and companies free to move production from plants in one country to those in others, it would be wise not to allow disparities in social and employment legislation to become too wide.

In short, while the battle between the advocates of big government at a European level and those of states' rights is a real one with genuine principles at stake, it is far from easy to know exactly where the line should be drawn. It will vary from issue to issue and from time to time and even the most consistent government will not always find itself on the same side of the argument.

There is, however, one matter that ought to unite everyone – namely the need to ensure that whatever is done at Community level is subject to equivalent accountability to that which applies at a national level. So far as the actions of ministers in the Council of Ministers are concerned, the responsibility must be with national parliaments, though it must be said that most have not yet found a satisfactory way of discharging it. Where the Council's decisions taken as a whole are concerned, the President in office should answer on its behalf to the European Parliament. That body already has the powers it needs for the task but has so far proved inept at carrying it out.

The result is a paradox. Though governments operating within a Community context are sharing their sovereignty they actually exercise it more freely from democratic control than when they enjoy its unfettered possession outside the Community context. For those who believe that, in whatever manner it is exercised and through whatever instruments, sovereignty flows from the people, this should be a matter of deep concern.

29

Deeper and Wider

Ernest Wistrich, 1992.

Ernest Wistrich is a former Director of the British Section of the European Movement.

THE European Community is on the threshold of major changes that could transform the present Common Market of twelve countries, based largely on intergovernmental co-operation, into an economic, monetary and political union organized on federal lines with a membership of 20 or more countries. How did we get to this stage, and why are these changes more likely now than in the past? Is the deepening of the Community into a federal European Union compatible with its enlargement to include most of the European Continent? And what type of a federation is likely to emerge?

The founders of the European Community, some 40 years ago, had as their ultimate aim a European federation. Their principal reasons were to prevent further European wars by creating supranational institutions, under which interdependence would erode unfettered national sovereignties and thus end the capacity of individual member states to wage war against each other. They chose diverse paths to their final objective. First there was the European Coal and Steel Community, formed in 1951, followed a year later by the European Defence Community and a parallel Political Community. When the latter failed to gain French ratification, the founders chose the economic road to union by creating the European Economic Community. Progress over the next 30 years was slow but, nevertheless, significant. The customs-free Common Market was completed ahead of time and, after the departure of President de Gaulle, who opposed supranational integration, the Community was enlarged. The European Parliament was directly elected and acquired control over the Community budget. There were two attempts at creating an economic and monetary union. The first failed after the oil crisis in 1973. The second established the European Monetary System as the first step to monetary union. Throughout this period the economies of the member states became increasingly interdependent, largely satisfying the hope of the founders that war between members would no longer be likely or possible.

What, then, are the current reasons for progress to union? They stem directly from the consequences of integration hitherto, but also as a result of the dramatic growth in global trade, capital flows and the development of new technologies which are making the concept of unfettered national economic sovereignty and the preservation of frontiers against free trade increasingly obsolete. The current speed-up of the process of integration was to correct the EEC's relative economic stagnation, as compared with the USA and Japan, caused after the 1973 oil crisis by protectionist policies of the member states of the EEC. It became clear that the EEC's relative decline would continue unless it created a single market able to compete on equal terms with its more successful competitors.

This was the principal motive for the Single European Act, aiming to create one economic area within which frontiers for goods, services, capital and people are to disappear by the end of this year. The Act, furthermore, recognized that a single market would not be complete until the major barriers of competing currencies were replaced by a single currency in a full monetary union. Such a union would not, however, work without economic convergence and measures of social cohesion that would protect the poorer regions and weaker sectors, threatened with further decline once national protection was removed. To achieve the Single Market by the end of 1992 required faster decisions than were obtainable by consensus. Qualified majority voting in the Council secured this. As a result, however, national democratic control over individual ministers could no longer be exercised. This role was transferred to the European Parliament which acquired co-decision powers with the Council on issues where majority voting applied. Finally, in recognition of the enhanced role of the emerging economic and monetary union in world affairs, common foreign and security policies were to be developed.

Although progress towards the objectives of the Single Act was taking place according to plan, external developments gave increased urgency to the process of deepening the Community. The collapse of the Communist system had far-reaching effects on the Community. First, there was German unification which resulted in that country becoming the Community's largest and richest state, capable of occupying a dominant position in Europe in the wake of the collapse of the Soviet empire. The fears of potential German domination, which led to the European Coal and Steel Community in the 1950s, were rekindled both in the East and the West. Even more than most of her Community partners, Germany recognized the danger of unfettered sovereignty and the temptations of ruling the roost. That is why Germany is the strongest protagonist of a political union within which her role would be subsumed in a federation and where the German voice would count for little more than that of its other constituent member states. This was the principal motive for the intergovernmental conference on political union. Indeed, Germany insists on political union as a price for accepting monetary union.

The next consequence of the ending of the East/West divide was that the status of neutrality, which kept several European countries from joining the Community, ceased to have much meaning. The six EFTA countries which were most anxious not to be excluded from the Single Market managed, after lengthy and difficult negotiations with the EC, to agree on a European Economic Area which would give them full access but no say over Community decisions. As soon as the Soviet Union abandoned control over Central and Eastern Europe, Austria applied for full membership, followed by Sweden and soon probably by most of the rest of the EFTA countries.

Then the Gulf crisis and the civil war in Yugoslavia exposed the weakness of the Community in arriving at common foreign and defence policies to deal with such issues and with those which could arise as a result of the growing Balkanization of the former Soviet empire. These experiences demonstrated that where the Community has competence, as on economic issues, it could act quickly and decisively by imposing trade embargoes and applying other economic sanctions. On foreign policy and defence there was no such consensus, with each member state pursuing its own national policies. Common positions were only arrived at with great difficulty and at the level of the lowest common denominator. The effect of compromises between conflicting perceptions of national foreign and defence traditions and interests have been clearly demonstrated: in the Gulf crisis only some countries sent troops; over the Yugoslav internal conflict, action by the Community was hampered by divergence over the recognition of the independence of the individual republics or the need to send peace-keeping forces. A common view is needed to promote and defend the interests of the Community as a whole, over the entire area of foreign and defence policies, and with it, a capacity to act on behalf of its members, as it already does over external relations in economic affairs.

Finally, there are the dramatic developments in Central and Eastern Europe where radical economic reforms towards the establishment of market economies, being socially divisive and painful, could undermine their still fragile democratic systems. The Community has recognized the dangers inherent in these changes and has already negotiated association agreements with Poland, Czechoslovakia and Hungary and provided economic aid to other countries in the area. Most of these countries look to the Community, not merely as a source of help and guidance in achieving market economies but as a haven of political stability for which they yearn. That is why most of them wish to join the Community as full members as soon as they can be admitted. In some ways, the need for political stability is seen as being more urgent than the inevitably lengthier process of adapting to a market economy. To secure that stability the Community will be under pressure to integrate these countries within its political framework even before their economies are ready to accept the full obligations of membership, while allowing them appropriately lengthy transitional arrangements for economic adaptation.

The perspective of the Community's enlargement to double its present size raises further issues about its management. Reaching unanimous decisions within the Community of 12 members is difficult and lengthy. That is why majority voting is increasingly being applied to new Community competences. Unanimity within a Community of 20 or more states is a certain recipe for stagnation, and no significant decisions in the common interest are likely to be reached except by compromises at the lowest common denominator. Indeed, failures to take common decisions could only lead to disillusionment and the possible collapse of the Community itself. The prospect of widening the Community by the admission of several countries before the end of this century therefore makes it imperative to change its decision-making processes to make it work.

What sort of Community will be needed to meet all the above challenges? It must become much more cohesive. As Winston Churchill put it 45 years ago, it needs to evolve into a form of United States of Europe, adapted to the specific needs and circumstances of its future member states. A federal system, based on the principle of subsidiarity, is surely the answer. In the European context, this requires the maximum of national and local autonomy to bring decision making down closer to people and thus help preserve the cultural identities of its diverse communities. European powers have to be confined to those responsibilities that need common decisions and management. A binding constitution, which guarantees maximum autonomy and self-government to the component parts of the federation, must be accompanied by reforms which make common decisions at federal level easier and quicker to reach. Effective democratic control over them demands full co-decision powers for the European Parliament. The Council of Ministers of 20 or more member states must take most decisions by majority. The Commission, the Community's executive organ, needs to be strengthened so that it has full powers of initiative over all Community competences. But its increased authority and powers must be made more democratically accountable. All its actions should be subject to effective control by the European Parliament. The President of the Commission should be elected by the Parliament on the recommendation of the Council of Ministers and his or her choice of individual commissioners subject to the Parliament's approval. In effect, the Commission would become a government that must have the confidence of the Parliament to continue in office. Finally, the new constitution that clearly allocates powers and responsibilities between the federal level and its constituent states must have suitable provisions for redress against the federal authority arrogating to itself powers that, under the principle of subsidiarity, should remain with the lower tiers of government. Final judgement would lie with the European Court of Justice as the arbiter of the constitution. The result would be a federation preserving all the cultural and linguistic values of its distinct and diverse national communities, exercising self-government and autonomy in all spheres in which European decisions are not needed. Not a super-state but a federation familiar to the Germans or the Swiss within their own countries. Will these changes happen?

Nothing is certain. But the shrinking world, the disintegrating Soviet empire, the desperate needs of the Third World and the common interests of Europeans require new structures if we are to prevent our Continent once again fragmenting into fully independent sovereign states that could so easily bring back the rivalries and conflicts which led to two world wars this century.

Index

Abacha, General, 137
Acheson, Dean, 73
Act of Settlement, 25
Acton, Lord-Power, abuse, 1-5
Adenauer, Konrad, 49
Adorno, Theodore, 168
Agrarian Confederation, 60
Africa 97, 127
Agriculture, 11, 210
   See also CAP
Air Transport, 98, 211
Algeria, torture, 110
Amazonian Indians, 166
America, 38, 41, 59, 60, 62-3, 108
   Constitution, 25
   Culture, 107
   Political relation, XIV
   Revolution, 65
   See also Unites States of America
Amsterdam, 108, 130
Anarchy, 38
Anglo American Empire - end, 83
Anglo Saxons, 26
Anti Market Campaign, 27
Anti Semitism, 197
Aquitaine, 145
Arabic, language, 146

Armani Suits, 109
Armenians, 149
Arms control, 70
Arms race, 214
Arnold, Mathew, Edmond Burke,
   Comments, XI
Asia, political relations, XIV
Ataturk, Kemel, 93
Athens, 145
Arts, 123
Atlantic, 40, 47, 99
   Alliance, 215
   Community, 215
   North, 99
   Ties, 78
   Sea Boards, 83, 97
Augustine, Saint, 147
Austria, 37, 100
   Eastern Europe, 9
   Economy, 9
   Exports, 9, 10
   Foreign Trade, 9
   Exports, 9, 10
   Government, 8
   Industry, 9, 10
   Migration, 12
   Schilling, 55

Australians, 42, 81
Authority, Wickedneess, Lord
    Action, 3

Balance of power, 40
Balkans, 146, 328
    Turkish involvement, 228
Baltic States, XIV, 3
Banks, 103
    European recovery, 48
    Central, 17, 51-2, 81
    England, XIV, 104
    France, 51
    Germany, 51
    Trade, 174
Barbarism, 37
Basle, International Settlement
    Bank, 55
Basque Country, 70, 96, 149, 195
Buadouin, King, 207
Bavaria, 91
Baudelaire, 192
Belgium, 16, 24, 56, 80
Benetton Jumpers, 109
Berlin, Free City, 70, 73
    Wall, Fall, 8, 73
Bevin, Ernest, Foreign Secretary,
    XV
Bill of Rights, 25, 33, 62, 65, 67, 106
Black Voters, 168
Blair, Tony, New Wilson?, 43
Body, Sir Richard, 2
Bosco, Henri, 132
Bossi, Umberto, 87
Brandel, Fernand, 108
Bretton Woods, 90
Britain, 25-35
    Constitution, XIV, 18, 21, 25-6
    Disease, 107
    Electorate, 28
    Democracy, 62
    Empire, 37, 42, 144
    Euro MPs, 79-80
    Europe, XI, XV, 24, 45
    Government, 25, 191
    Identity, 109

India, 37
    Parliament, X
    Service Men, 207
    Social Services, 76
    Sovereignty, 27, 77
    Tolerance, 106
    Universities, 94
British Airport Authority, 179
    See also Air Travel
Britain, Sir Leon, 22-3
Bruges Group, 19, 27, 82
    See Also Margaret Thatcher
Brussels, 17, 20, 28-9, 31-2, 88, 113,
    117, 121, 149, 151-2
    Economic and Social Committee,
        179
    Transport Forum, 180
    Treaty, 214
Budapest, 97, 112,
    1956, 133
Buddhism, 147
Bulgaria, XIV
Bull, George, XVII
Bullock, Lord, Study Hitler, Stalin,
    3-4
Bundesbank, 51, 104
Burberry Raincoats, 109
Burke, Edmond, 146, 202
    Arnold, Comments, XI
Bureaucracy, 17, 21, 27, 96, 98
    Europe, 193, 209
Burns, Robbie, 41
Burroughs William, 168
Busek, Erhard, 7
Business - Management, 5
Burt, Ronald, XIII, 15, 25
Byzantium, 42

CAP see Common Agricultural
    Policy
Calvinism, 200, 202-3
Canada, 42, 66
Canals, 98
Cannon-Brookes, Peter, XII
Capitalism, 99
Carlyle, Thomas, 36-7, 41

Carter, Jimmy, 60, 220
Cartesian Route - Monetary Union, 51
Casanova, 132
Catalan - Spain
  Autonomy, 87
  Language, 134
Cathedrals, England, 206
Catholicism, 62, 67, 196, 200, 202-3
Caxton, William, 205
Celac, Sergiv, XV, XVI
Celts, 206
Central and European Countries (CEECS), XV, XVI, 7, 9, 12-3, 44, 155
Central Bank, 23, 56, 81
  Europe, 17, 55, 101
  Swiss, 55
Chaban-Delmas, J. 121
Charlemagne - Empire, 30, 98, 147
Charles, 11, 66, 200
Charles V, 98
Chaucer, Geoffrey, 41, 205
Chief Seattle, 166
China, 99
Chinese Proverb - Patriotism, XIV
Christian Democracy, 80, 86
Christianity, 109, 147, 206
Churches - England, 206
Churchill, Winston, 44, 70, 91, 117
  United States of Europe, 146
Cicero, 132
City of London, XVIII, 211
Civil Rights, 61, 110, 170
Civilised Society, 206
Civil Wars
  Europe, 116
  Spain, 133, 163
  USA, 83
  Yugoslavia, 228
Civilisation, 37
Clarke, Kenneth - Treasury, XIV
Class War, 163, 166
Clive of India, 37
Coal and Steel Community, XV
Cockfield, Lord, 28-30, 32

Coca Cola, 176
Cold War, 86
Coleman, John, 35
Collectivism, 124
College of Europe, 205
Colonialism, 95, 110, 207
  Europe, 110
  De-colonialism, 110
COMECON, 47
Common Agricultural Policy, 19, 80, 113, 210, 222
Common Currency, 56, 81
Common European Home, 151-7
Common Market, XV, 47, 138
Communism, 11, 123, 20, 46-7, 109, 188, 227
  Post-Communism, 47, 54, 193
Community - Enlargement, 229
Community - Majority Voting, 229
Confederation, 19
Common Foreign Policy, 22-3
Companies, Multinational, 79
Congress of Vienna 1815, 44
Conservative Party, XVIII, 31, 178
Constant, Benjamin, 200
Copernicus, 147
Council of Europe, 48, 70, 72, 137
Council of Ministers, 27, 32, 52, 82, 180, 223, 231
Corporate Success, 5
Creative Writing, 97
Creighton, Bishop, 1
Crespo, M., 187
Crimean War, 36-7
Criminal Courts - International, 75
  Nuremburg Principles, 173
Criminal Justice System, 60
Cromwell, Oliver, 38, 41
Crusades, 36
Culture, 97, 168, 197
  Anthropology, 110
  Foreign, 122
  Global, 109
  History, XIII
  Identity, 230
  International, 108

White, 111, 171
Custom Posts, 212
Cyprus, XIV, 110
Czechoslovakia, 46, 100,112
  Czech Republic, XIV, 119
  Austrian Exports, 9
  Migration, 12

Dahrendorf, Ralph, XVII, 45
Daily Telegraphy, 59
Daley, Janet, XIII, 59
Darre, Walter, Nazi Agriculture
  Minister, 166
Darwin, Charles, 41
Davies, Christie, 65
De Compostela, Santiago, 134
Defence, Europe, 193, 318
Deflation, 52
De Gaulle, Charles, 82, 84, 134,
  217, 222
Dell, Edmund, XIV
Delors, Jacques, 117, 154, 157, 184,
  188
Denmark, 30, 87, 206
Democracy, 28, 117, 118
  Europe, 3
Derby, Lady, 38
Descartes, 129
Deutschmark, 49
Developing Countries, 213
Dickens, Charles, 111, 124
Diderot, 129
Diplomacy, XV, 4
Disraeli, Benjamin, 147, 167
Dollar, 46, 54
Donizetti, Gaetano, 91
Downing Street, 28, 37
Drake, Sir Francis, 41, 65-6
Drugs, 212
Dublin, 23, 112
Dubrovnik - Praxis Meeting, 112
Dumas, Alexandrie, 149
Dumas, Roland, 24
Dunn, Ted, 69
Dunn, Waldo Hilary, 44
Dutch, 66-68, 97

Pen Club, 133
See also Netherlands

ECU, 54, 212
  Treasury Bonds, 174
EEC, 35, 45, 96, 146
EFTA Countries, 47, 193, 228
EMS, 54, 174
EMU, 51, 52, 56
ERM, XIV, 90, 103, 186, 187, 219
EU see European Union
Eastern Block, 76, 122
Eastern Europe, XV, XVI, 4, 7, 9,
  46-7, 72, 74, 76, 96, 112, 118,
  156, 188
Eastern Germany, 153
  Uprising, 46
Eastern Markets, 9
  Austria, 9, 10
Economic and Monetary Union,
  See EMU
Economic and Social Committee,
  179
Economic Configuration, Europe,
  XIII
Economic Liberation, 81
Economic Progress, 99
Economics, Transition, 12
Economist, 137
Economy, Europe, 188-189
Egypt, 40
Ellemann - Jenson, Uffe, 87, 88
Emanvelle, Vittorio, 85
Elizabeth, Queen, 36
Empire - British, 42, 144
Economic and Monetary Union
  See EMU
England and English, 37, 41-2
English Channel, Continent, 40
English Colonies, 39
English History, Reformation, 35
English Statesmen, 40
Entrepreneurs, 52, 202
Equal Rights, 61
Equality, 164
Estonians, 119

Ethnocide, 171
Euro Arab Dialogue, 121
Euro Fanatics, 28, 30
Euro Federalists, 63
Euro Standards, 176
Euro Technocrats, 30
Europe and Nigeria, 137
Exchange Rate Mechanism
    See ERM
Europe, 21st Century, 86, 92
    Britain's Role, XI
    Civil War, 116
    Common Heritage, 119, 195
    Common Defence, 57, 86, 193
    Enlargement, 6-7, 9, 11-13
    Family of Nations, XII, 216
    Freedom, 111
    Future, XII
    History, 96
    Identity, IX, XII, 6, 63, 111, 197
    Internal Market, 186
    Languages, 127
    Liberation, 207
    Nationalism, XII, III
    Nuclear Deterrent, 22
    Political Relations, 174
    Political Union, 19
    Re-unification, 152-4
    Single Currency, XIII, 17, 32
    Single Market, XIII, 8, 28-9, 178-
        9, 184, 187, 210, 212, 219, 222,
        227
    Social Dimensions, 184
    Social Engineering, 116
    Sovereign States, 2, 54, 61, 102
    Structure, 70 - 73
    Study Groups, 183-4
    Sutherland Committee 185-6
European Alliances, 41
European Central Bank, 56, 81, 141,
    211
European Civilisation, 123, 128
European Commission, 121, 126,
    180
European Committee of the
    Regions, 185, 186

European Coal and Steel
    Community, 48, 226, 227
European Community, XI, I, 2,15,
    17-20, 27-8, 53, 68, 86, 208 -209
European Councils, 13, 209
European Court of Justice, 231
European Culture, XII, 126 -28,
    146-7, 149, 232
European Currency, 186, 219
European Destiny, 27
European Economic Community,
    35, 45, 96, 146, 152
European Elections, 28
European Family, 70
European Federation, 29, 59, 82
European Free Trade Areas, 112, 174
European Law, 190
European League of Economic Co-
    operation, 45, 110
European Parliament, 17, 18, 20, 32,
    33, 184
European Political Union, 16, 54
European Security, 161
European Snake, 53
European Social Chapter, 47, 71
European Superstate, XVII, 54, 81,
    209, 218, 220
European Train, 189-190
EuropeanTreaties, X, 111
Europeanism, 196
Evans, Douglas, 77
Exhibition 1951, 36
Export Led Growth, 89

Falklands Campaign, 76, 78
Fanaticism, Political, 109
Family, Breakdown, 171
Far East, 108, 176
Fascists, 159
Federal Europe, XIV, 3, 5, 17, 18,
    21, 23, 30, 31
Federalism, 29, 61, 62, 79, 82, 102,
    193, 218, 225
    Germany, 231
    Switzerland, 231
Fernandez, Dominique, 129

Fidel Castro, 165
Film Making, 97
  Germany, 109
  Holywood, 60, 109
  Italy, 109
Ferranti, Basil de, 102
Finance, 99
  Services, 212
  Institutions, 223
Finland, 155
Flanders, 16, 87
Folk Lore, 123
Football, Europe, 88
Foreign Office, Mandarins, XV
Fortress Europe, 72, 81, 174, 175,
  196
France, 37, 40-1, 68, 82, 136
  Constitution, 25
  Currency, 49
  History, 94
  Republic, 49, 68, 80, 97, 106, 134
  Revolution, 42, 62, 84
  Socialist Government, 189
  Traditions, 79, 96, 97, 131
France and Germany, 16, 24, 51,
  116, 188-9
Franco, 131
Freedom, 36, 124
Freedom of Information, 106
Free Speech, 170
Free Trade Area, 43, 78, 81, 174
Freud, Sigmund, 106
Frontier Controls, Europe, 212
Froude, James Anthony, 35, 38, 43

GATT (General Agreement on
  Tarrifs), 175, 178, 186, 213
GEMU, 55
GMP Gross National Product), 69
Genghis Khan, 206
George, Eddie, Bank of England,
  XIV
Genocide, 171
Germany, 130-1
  Culture, 107
  Monetary Union, 55, 90

  Place in Europe, 80
  Unification, 191
Germany and France, 16, 24, 51,
  116, 188-9
Gibbon, Edward, 200
Gibraltar, Rock, 39
Giscard, d'Estaing, 51
Global Economy
  see World Economy
Gladstone, William, 38
Glasnost, 69
Global Environment, 78
  Economic, 79, 104, 108
  Culture, 110
Global Homogeneity, 171
Global Trading, XIV, 79, 81
Goethe's Weimar, 50
Gonzalez, Felipe, 134
Gorbachov, Michael, XII, 76, 112,
  133
  Brize Norton, 118, 160
  Disarmament, 75
  European Family, 70, 72
  Glasnost, 69
  Sinatra Doctrine, 46
Governance, 27
Grass, Günter, 130
Granville, Lord, 38
Great Powers, 40
Greece, 30, 41, 106
Guest Workers, 98
Gulf War, 228

Hague, William, XVIII, 141
Hallstein, Walter, 86
Hama, Noriko, XVII, 85
Hamburg, 108
Hapburg Empire, 97, 98
  Spanish, 66
  Turkish, 146
Harrod, Roy, 52
Hartington, Lord, 38
Hastings, Warren, 37
Havel, Vaclev, XV, XVI, 130, 134
Heath, Edward, 29, 44, 151
Health and Safety, 187

Helsinki Accord, 214
Helsinki Act, 22
Henry II, 147
Henry VIII, 36
Heseltine, Michael, 5
Hinduism, 147
History, Culture, XIII
Hitler, Adolf, 44, 65, 98
Hoggart, Richard, 93, 110
Hollywood, Films, 60, 109
    Film Making, 97, 109
Holocaust, 95, 99, 167, 168
Holy Roman Empire, 160
Hong Kong, 56, 108
Homogeneity, 63
House of Commons, 18, 25, 164,
    183
House of Lords, 25, 183
Howell, David, XII, 101
Huguenots, 200
Human Rights, 71, 112, 164
    EU, 71, 206
Hungary, 46, 100, 118
    Austrian Exports, 9
    Migration, 12
Hurd, Douglas, 15, 17, 21, 22
Huxley, Thomas, 41

IRA, 212
Iberian Peninsula, 30
Iceland, 146
Ideology, 118
Identity, 7
    Europe, IX, XII, 7, 63, 197
Industrial Archaeology, 164
Ignatieff, Michael, X, XI, 93, 105
Imperialism, 98
    Asia, 111
    Europe, 110
Income Tax, 65
Immigrants, 167
Individualism, 99, 124, 172
India, 37, 99
    Indian Mutiny, 37
Indonesians, 94
Industrial Revolution, 201-2

Inventions, 201
Industry, 99, 177
Integrated Europe, XIV, 102
International Affairs, 4, 159, 171-2,
    178
Investment, Far East, 175
Ireland, 41, 80, 196
    North, 196
Islam, 147
    see also Moslems
Italy, 16, 24, 37, 41, 79, 80, 85, 97,
    132, 134
    Alps, 87
    Northern, 97

James 11, 66
Japan, 81, 99
Jay, Lord, X
Jenkins, Lord, 28, 30
Jews, 147
Johnson, Douglas, XI, 93, 110
Johnson, Lydon, 44
Joan of Arc, 148
Jones, Lynne, 3
Joyce, James, 111, 129

Kent, Bruce, 164
Kenya, 110
Keynes, John Maynard, 52
Kinnock, Neil, 28
Kohl, Helmut, 80, 84
Konrad, George, 111
Kohr, Leopold, Breakdown of
    Nations, 44
Kundera, Milan, 111, 195
Kuwait, Invasion, 4

Labour, Division, 200
Labour, Legislation, 117
Labour Party, X, 28, 30
Landes, David, 200
Latin America, 66, 99
Latvia, XIV
Law, 190
Lawson, Nigel, XVII
League of Nations, 117

Leadership, 104, 157
Leningrad, 112
Lewis, Flora,XII, 115
Liberal Democrats, 164-5
Liberalism, 98-9, 168-70, 213,
Liberty, 36
Lifestyles, 98
Lincoln, Abraham, 60
Lithuania, XIV
Lloyd-Hughes, Trevor, 42
Lockean Idealists, 61
London, 108, 111
  East End, 165-6
London School of Economics, 19
Los Angles, 108
Louis XIV, 67
Luther's Eisenach, 50
Lukaszewski, Professor, 205
Luxemburg, 56, 80

MEP see Members of the European
  Parliament
Maastricht Treaty, 1, 85, 87-9, 91-2,
  138, 185, 187-8, 190, 193
Macaulay, Thomas, 41, 201-2
McKendrick, Neil, 200
MacMillan, Harold, XIV, 52
McPherson, Mr, US Treasury, 176
Magna Carta, 25, 62, 206
Mahler Gustave, 147
Malaysia, 110
Management, 5, 99
Mann, Thomas, 129
Marx, Karl, 91, 171
Markets, 177
Marshall Plan, 70-5, 88
Mastnak,Tomaz, 3
Marlborough, Duke, 67
Mayr, Johann Simon, 91
Mediterranean, XIII, 71, 108, 132,
  134, 197, 203
Mendes - France, Pierre, 49
Members European Parliament, 17-
  18, 20
Meritocracy, 172
Mexico City, 66

Middle Classes, 164, 168
Mirabeau, Gabreil Riqueti, 202
Michelangelo, 132
Middle Ages, 131
Migration, 12-3
  Austria, 12
  Czech Republic, 12
  Europe, 116
  Hungary, 12
  Poland, 12
  Slovakia,12
Military Presence, USA- Europe, 81
Mill, John Stuart, 41, 202
Minerva Owl, XVII, 91
Mitterrand, Francois, 157
Modernity, XIII
Mollet, Guy, 134
Monnet, Jean, 56, 101, 116, 121
Moscow, 112
Moslems, 94
  See also Islam
Motorways, 99
  See also Transport
Mozart, 149
Multinational Companies, 79, 184
Murphy's Law, 53
Museums, 99, 109
Museum Culture, 123

NATO, XII, 22, 73, 78, 178, 213
  German Membership, 49
Napoleon, 44, 65, 79, 98, 190
Natal, 42
National Defence-Europe, 57
National Governments, 8
National Markets, 177
Nationalism, 31, 46, 98, 147
  Europe, 109, 209
National Socialists, 3
National Sovereignty, 28, 194
  See also Sovereign States
Nation States, 99
  Europe, 115-9, 153, 191-2, 194-5,
  218
Navigation Acts, 83
Nazis, 95-6, 159

Netherlands, 52, 66-7, 80, 130
See also Dutch
Nevada, 63
New European, IX, X, XI, XVI,
163
New Labour, XVIII, 170
Newsweek, Journal, XVI
New World, 39, 42
New York, 45, 63, 146
Nicholson, Baroness, 164
Nicholson, Harold, 93
Nieuwenhuijze, C.A.O. van, 121
Nigeria, 137 -146
Business Community, 143
Christians, 139-40
Independence, 138
Moslems, 140
Oil Refineries, 139
Nigeria and Europe, 137
Norman England, 206
North Atlantic Alliance, XII, 160-1
North Atlantic Treaty, 214
Nixon, Richard, 53
Nooteboom, Cess, XIII, 129
North Sea, 71
Norway, 132
Nuclear Weapons, 160-1
Deterrent, 12, 64, 214
Europe, 2, 57
See also Wars

OECD, 47
Official Version, Argentine, Film, 163
Orange Men, 68
Oguntimoju, Dele, 137
Orwell, George, Spanish Civil War,
129
Ottoman Empire, 97
Ovid, 132

Pacific Basin, 94
Pacific Rim, 108
Pandora's Box, 91-2
Paris, 111
Parliament, Democracy
Debate, X

Government, 26, 32
Palmerston, Lord, 37
Pearson Kenneth Leech, XIII, 145
Patriotism, Chinese Proverb, XIV
Philip II, Spain, 66
Pike, Sir Michael, 2
Plantagenet Princes, 41
Pohl, Kark, Bundesbank, 51
Poland, XIV, 46, 97, 112
Austrian Exports, 9
Migration, 12
Political Culture, 106
Political Relations, America, XIV
Political Relations, XIV
Political Terminology, 219
Political Correctness, 168, 170
Politicians, 36
Popes, 36
Pius XII
Portugal, 80, 97, 106
Imperialism, 98
Post Modernity, 192
Poverty, 167, 170
Powell, Enoch, XV, 151, 159
Power, 3, 70
Decentralised, 70
Lord Acton, 1-5
Prague, 111, 130, 145
1968, 133
Pravda, 93
Praxis Meeting, Dubrovnik, 112
Presley, Elvis, 108
Propaganda, X, 4
Protestantism, 67, 99, 202
Work Ethic, 203
Proust, Marcel, 129
Prussia, 97

Queen Mary, 206

Racism, 165, 167-9
Europe, 110, 197
Policies, 66
Railways, 98
Raleigh, Sir Walter, 41
Rankin, Aidan, 163

Reagan, Ronald, 60, 82, 220
Reciprocity, 175-6
Reformation, 35, 98
Regional Authorities, 8
Regional Markets, 177
Religions, 98
Renaissance, 98
Revolution, 36, 38
    England 1688, 65
Ridley, Nicholas, 5
Rilke, Rainer Maria, 129
Rippon, Geoffrey, XIV, 173
Rivers, Danube, Rhine, 98
Robinson, Anne, XIV, 179
Roman Catholics, 67-8
Roman Empire, 206
    Fall, 35
Romania XIV, 118
Rome, 132
Rousseau, Jean Jacques, 200
Royal Air Force, 207
Russia, 40, 74, 97, 119
    Eastern Front, 133
    Elite, 112
    Empire, 133
    See also Soviet Union

Saar Territory, 48-9, 55-6
Saddam Hussein, 4
Salazar, Antonio de Olivera, 106
Salzburg, 145
Saxons, 206
Say's Law (Jean Baptiste Say), 201
Scandinavia, 155
Schiller, Johann, 51
Schlesinger, Philip, XIII
Schumann Plan, XIV
Science, 124
Scotland, 41, 70, 191-2, 195, 200,
    202-3
    Nationalism, 32
Sebastopol, 37
Security, 176
Seneca, 132
Serfdom, 202
Sex Discrimination, 61

Single Currency, XIII, 17, 32
Single European Act, 78, 177, 220,
    226
Single Market, XIII, 8, 28-9, 103,
    173, 178-9, 184, 187, 210, 212,
    219, 222, 227
Shakespeare, William, 41, 111
Singapore, 65, 99
Sked, Alan, 19, 20
Slaverhoff, Dutch Poet, 133
Slovenia, XIV
Slovakia, XIV
    Austrian Exports, 9
    Migration, 12
Smith, Adam, 201
Smith, F. E., 202
Smithers, Sir Peter, 137-8, 142
Social Chapter, 47, 71
Soros,George, 49
South Americans, 42
Sovereignty, 2, 56, 60, 96, 104, 117,
    194, 219, 223, 227
Sovereign States, 2, 54, 61, 102
Soviet Union, 4, 75-6, 118-9, 138,
    143, 153-4, 160, 191, 214
    Borders, 47
    Embassy, 93
    Empire, 227
    National Minorities, 31, 82, 111
    Satellites, 109
    See also Russia
Spaak, Paul Henry, 214
Spain, 97, 132
    Armada, 65
    Civil War, 133, 163
    Imperial, 65, 80, 98
Spitzbergen, 146
Stalin, Joseph, 44
Stendhal, Henri Marie Beyle, 129
Staunton, George, 170-1
Stone, Norman, XIII, 199
Strasbourg, 113
Streeter, Gary, 164
Strindberg, Johan August, 129
Subsidiarity, 3, 21, 92
    See also Federalism

Sudan, 95
Super state- Europe, XVIII, 18, 23,
  194
Survival - International, 165, 171
Sutherland Committee, 185-6
Sweden, 55, 132
Switzerland, 70, 199-200
  Central Bank, 55
  Confederation, 147
Sydney, 146

Tacitus, 132
Taparelli, Massimo D'Azeglio, 85
Tariffs, 53
Taxation, 63
Technology, 124, 226
Television, 109
Telecommunications, 211
Teresa, Mother, 148
Terrorists, 134, 212
  IRA, 212
Thatcher, Margaret, XII, XIV, 15,
  21, 22, 24, 27, 28, 71, 77-84, 102,
  106, 117, 126, 157, 173-4, 205
  Bruges Speech, 127, 174, 178
Third Republic, France, 203
Third Way, Myth, 47
Third World, 95-6, 109-110, 231
  Culture, 111, 165
Times, Newspaper, XVI, 43, 59, 137
Tokyo, 45, 108
Tocqueville, Alexis de, 202
Torture, Prevention, 110
  Algeria, 110
Toryism, One Nation, 167, 168
  Euro MPs, 31
Totalitarian Systems, 130
Trade, 99
  Free Trade, 155
  Commodities, 176
  Liberalisation, 178
  World, 174
Trade Unions, 182
  Transport, 101
  Air Services, 98, 180
  Canals, 98

Motorways, 98, 180
Problems, 98
Railways, 98
UK-Europe, 180
Treaty of Rome, 92, 156, 180, 186,
  206, 211
Tribalism, 95, 116, 192
Tudor Princes, 41
Tugendhat, Christopher, XII, 100,
  217
Turgot, A. R. J, 84
Turkey, XIV,37, 40-1
  Guest Workers, 98
Tyndall, John, 41

UNESCO, 94, 127
USA, see United States of America
USSR, see Soviet Union
Ulster, Orange Men, 68
United Europe, 3, 27
Unites States of America, 59, 88, 96,
  134, 207
  Constitution, 83
  Military, 81
  See Also America
United Kingdom, see Britain
United Nations, 71, 75
United States of Europe, 16, 82,
  102, 146
Universal Suffrage, 33
Universities, British, 94
Urals, 142

VAT, 63
Vaevlik, Ludvik, 130
Vatican, 132
Vladivostock, 112
Voltaire, Francois, 200

Wales, 179, 195
  Welsh Office, 180
Wallas, Graham, 4
Wallonia, 16, 87
Wars, 31
  Europe, 17
  First World War, 112, 116, 207

Religious, 109
Second World War, 8, 116, 118, 169-71
Tribal, 31
Warsaw, 97, 111
Warsaw Pact, 160
Washington, 60-1
Washington, George, 38
Welles, Orson, Third Man, 199-200
Westpolitik, XVI
Welfare, 99, 125
Western Civilisation, 122
Europe, 72-3, 75-6, 118
Westminster, 27, 32-3, 149
William, Sir Brandon Rys, 45-6, 52, 55
William of Orange, 66-8, 206
Wilson, Harold, XIV, 43, 134
Wistrich, Ernest, XIII, 225

Women's Movements, 61
World Economy, XIV, 212
World Trade, 178
World War,
First, 112, 116, 207
Second, 8, 116, 118, 169-71
Workers Rights, 81
Working Class, British, 108, 164-5, 167, 168, 171

Xenophobia, 165, 172

Yalta Conference, 44
Yen, 46
Yugoslavia, 2-3, 83, 138, 143, 196
Civil War, 228
Guest Workers, 98

Zeebrugge Ferry Disaster, 205